Soldiers and Power

Soldiers and Power

The Development Performance of the Nigerian Military Regime

Victor A. Olorunsola

HOOVER INSTITUTION PRESS   1977

Stanford University   •   Stanford, California

Hoover Institution Publication 168

International Standard Book Number: 0-8179-6681-1
Library of Congress Catalog Card Number: 76-48485
Printed in the United States of America

For my mother

and

the Anders

CONTENTS

LIST OF TABLES

LIST OF TABLES

PREFACE

The basic concern of this book is the development performance of the military as viewed from various vantage points: first, the vantage point of the consumers of the governmental policies and output; second,
the military regime's perception of its own performance; and, finally, the objective measure of performance. The point to remember is that an objective
development performance record by itself is insuffi-
cient. It could be argued that a perception of high
performance by the consumers, even when not supported
by significant objective data, may be salutary to
development. Similarly, high performance attainment
as seen from a strictly "objective" vantage point can
be seriously undermined in the face of low subjective
performance ratings.

I believe that my modest contribution and the
uniqueness of my effort reside in the position that
the development performance of military regimes should
be viewed from various vantage points. Moreover, we
must not a priori take the position that African military are not agents of development. Nor should we
accept the reverse to be true in the absence of hard
evidence. It is certainly inadequate and grossly
deficient to ignore the perceptions of the domestic
"consumers" of governmental policies and output, as
well as those of influential segments of society and
military rulers, even though the latter may be self-
serving. Valid theories and postulates about African
military rulers and their development capabilities
will emerge only after a series of comprehensive case
studies of African military regimes' performance has
been undertaken. I trust that this analysis of
Nigeria's Gowon regime initiates a move in the right
direction.

It is neither necessary nor particularly helpful
to develop a complicated model. A simple conceptual
framework that lucidly outlines and justifies the

the study, the assumptions, the criteria, and the mea-
surements to be used is all that is needed at this
stage. I have not addressed myself to the early years
of the Gowon regime (1967-70) because those were the
civil war years when the primary and all-consuming
effort of the military was seen and accepted as the
prosecution of the civil war.

The reader also needs to be warned that my goal
is not that of writing a political history of the
country. Nor am I particularly interested in the economic and political history of Nigeria. In two different books—*The Politics of Cultural Sub-Nationalism in
Africa* and *Political Reconstruction in Two African States*—I
dealt with Nigerian political history and discussed
the political dynamics and factors operating in the
social system. In addition, there are no new contributions that can be made in view of the excellent col-
lective contributions of Professors E. O. Awa, James
Coleman, Kalu Ezera, John P. Mackintosh, Richard Sklar,
and Margery Perham. Readers interested in Nigerian
political history and dynamics should consult the
works of these authors noted in the bibliography.

Most Nigerians are quick to point out that the
Gowon regime had greater resources available to it
than did the governments that preceded it. In addition, the civilian regime of Tafawa Balewa did not
survive to complete its five-year development scheme.
Given the uniqueness of colonial systems, however,
it is not particularly productive to compare colonial
government's achievement with that of an indigenous
government. In any case, it could be argued that that
is not the real issue. At the very least, then, com-
parisons can be invidious. To engage in outlandish
comparison under the circumstance is to run the high
risk of creating distortions in perspectives. I
sparingly, judiciously, and carefully juxtapose performances of different regimes only when distortions
can be avoided or satisfactorily explained. The
reader should note chapters 5 and 6.

For those interested primarily in the economic
conditions and growth of Nigeria, I recommend the bibliography, which contains the relevant works of Professors O. Aboyade, H. M. Onitiri, G. K. Helleiner,
and Peter Kilby and Mr. Ayida.

I cannot overemphasize the fact that my concern

is not with growth per se but with the "incidence of
growth" or distributive equity, which I call development. In other words, I asked myself: Who benefits
from growth? Who is perceived as benefiting from
growth? In the Nigerian context, does military rule
concern itself primarily with the well-being of the
majority of its citizens? Does the common Nigerian
believe that the Gowon regime is catering to his economic needs and well-being? To ask these, in the
Nigerian case at least, is not to impose a value.
Rather, it is to accept the goals set by the Gowon
regime.

For a long time political scientists and histori-
ans have recognized the importance of newspapers as a
legitimate data source. Many economists, however, may
regard them either as an inelegant or as an unorthodox
data source. Some may even hold them in irreverence.
Nevertheless, given the objective of this research,
the contemporary nature of the data sought, and the
time factor, this source had to be used. Although the
New Nigerian and the *Daily Times* may not be the *Wall Street
Journal* or the *New York Times*, I believe I have made a
strong case in chapter 1 for the validity of their
use. I am hopeful that some economists will be convinced.

The writing of this manuscript as well as a substantial part of the research for it was made possible
by the award of a National Fellowship during 1974-75
from the Hoover Institution on War, Revolution, and
Peace. Some of the data used were gathered in 1971-72
under the financial auspices of the Ford Foundation,
the Social Science Research Council, and the International Development and Research Center of Indiana
University. I am grateful to all these organizations
for their financial support.

A number of specialists and staff members of the
Hoover Institution have been particularly supportive
in various ways. Although it is not possible to name
them all, I would like to single out Drs. Peter
Duignan and L. H. Gann, Ms. Iris Boudart, Karen Fung,
Marie Schutz, Ellen Leung, Mary Gilmor, and Dorothy
Godsall. Outside the Hoover Institution, I should
mention Ali and Molly Mazrui, Donald and Edith
Rothchild, and Francis Duignan. I am also grateful
to Marya Donch, who cared to decipher and type the
first draft of the manuscript.

Last, but not least, I would like to thank my family—Carol, Ade, and Michael—for their incredible tolerance of a "rolling stone."

Of course the sins of omission and commission are properly mine and mine alone.

Victor Olorunsola
Stanford University
April 24, 1975

CHAPTER ONE

*Framework for the Study of Development Performance
of African Military Regimes*

"The wind of change is sweeping through Africa,"
Harold Macmillan said in a famous speech. Clearly,
the British prime minister was referring to the rise
of African nationalism and the resolve of Africans to
exchange rule by European colonial masters for self-
government and independence. At that time the possibility, let alone the probability, of direct involvement of the military in the politics of sub-Saharan
Africa was not self-evident. As a matter of fact,
with the exception of Sudan's military takeover in
November 1958, the supplantation of African civilian
administration with military rule did not occur until
1965, beginning with Congo Kinshasa (November 25, 1965),
and Dahomey (December 22, 1965), then Central African
Republic (January 1, 1966), Upper Volta (January 3,
1966), Nigeria (January 15, 1966, July 29, 1967),
Ghana (February 24, 1966, January 13, 1967), Togo
(January 13, 1967), Sierra Leone (March 22, 1967),
Congo Brazzaville (August 4, 1968), and Mali
(November 19, 1969), to mention a few.

By and large scholars were caught by surprise,
for, given the nature and role of the colonial army
in Africa, it would have been impossible to accurately
forecast a political leadership role for the African
military. In the confrontation between the colonial-
ists and nationalists one could not say that African
soldiers were squarely on the side of the nationalists
(with the possible exception of Algeria). Nor can one
categorically state that the African military constituted the repository for highly technical and differ-
entiated skills useful for modernization and development. It was clear that the civilian bureaucracy, not
the military bureaucracy—such as it was, constituted
the reservoir of knowledge and skilled manpower.
Moreover, we must recall that much was made of the

Westminster model or other "metropolitan" models, and their bright future in Africa was assumed.

Thus, while the recency of the phenomenon of military involvement in politics is partially responsible for the short history of research in this field, a number of assumptions about military regimes contributed to the preoccupation with studies of the politics of coup d'etat.

Many scholars found the rapidity of these coups d'etat alarming. Some were disturbed because they raised the specter of gross political instability. There probably existed a general reluctance to admit that one's prognosis had proved wrong. So, for a variety of reasons Africanists shared an extremely skeptical, if not antagonistic, attitude toward this chain of events. It is probably this attitude more than any other factor that is responsible for the overwhelming preoccupation with studies dealing with the whys and wherefores of military overthrow. If one has little or no confidence in the ability of the military as political functionaries, and if one is convinced that they are usurpers of power, then it is not unreasonable to concentrate upon researching ways to prevent the mushrooming of military regimes. The presumption is that if we can delineate the reasons for coups d'etat, then civilian leaders—out of enlightened self-interest, at least—can and will work hard to eradicate these causes.

The explanations for coups d'etat have run the whole gamut from factors endogenous to the military organizations to exogenous factors, down through personality factors.[1] The problem is that, as far as sub-Saharan Africa is concerned, these theories of military intervention have not been very rewarding: the many exceptions have seriously weakened their predictive validity.

To be more specific, let us consider some of these explanations:

   1. *Size of the military as a cause of coup d'etat.*

      The Central African Republic, with a total armed force of 1,100, has a military regime; Nigeria, with a total military force of a quarter of a million, is under military rule.

2. *Primordial factors as a cause of coup d'etat.*

Somalia is characterized by ethnic homogene-
ity, Burundi by ethnic polarization, Dahomey
and Zaire by ethnic fragmentation. All of
these countries have experienced a military
takeover.

3. *Poor economy as a cause of military coup d'etat.*

Libya has a per capita income of $1,500, and
Upper Volta's GNP per capita is $40. Neither
country has been spared a military takeover.

4. *Contagion, or the so-called demonstration effect.*

The Ivory Coast is bounded by Ghana, Upper
Volta, and Mali; Tanzania by Zaire and
Uganda. Yet in none of these countries has
the civilian administration been supplanted
with military rule.

At best we are left with a plethora of plausible
causation. In the meantime military regimes continue
to multiply in Africa. A reorientation is therefore
imperative.

We can take military involvement in politics in
a Huntingtonian sense; that is, the military gets involved in politics for the same reasons that the
clergy, students, and labor do.[2]   In that case there
is nothing highly unusual about military involvement
in the politics of changing societies. One could then
argue that our efforts would be better spent on study-
ing the actual governments run by the military. It
may well be, as some have suggested, that different
professional groupings bring differing styles, skills,
and capabilities to the tasks of governance and that
these affect policy choices and societal output.[3] Al-
ternatively, one might view military involvement in
politics in the same light as most African military
governments view it. In that case military governments are corrective regimes. Consequently, we need
to be concerned in comparative analysis with how various military regimes compare with their civilian pre-
decessors. In short, how well have they performed as
corrective regimes?

However one proceeds, there is a necessity for

a shift in scholarly emphasis away from the study of
coups d'etat to the study of military regimes and
their performance. The whole issue whether military
intervention is an automatically dysfunctional phenomenon in Africa is ultimately an empirical question.
The point needing emphasis is not that the study of
military intervention in Africa should cease forthwith
but that serious case studies of the performance of
military regimes in Africa should be intensified. How
should the performance of military regimes in Africa
be studied, and what are the advantages of this kind
of approach?

It must be conceded at the outset that we now
have a few studies that have concentrated, not on the
politics of the coup d'etat, but on the alleged capabilities of military regimes in Africa. Yet the few
who have studied military performance have in general
looked at it only from one vantage point.[4] This is a
mistake because the consumers of public policies, as
well as the formulators and executors of these policies, are an important factor in the performance
equation.

Parenthetically I should note that there are
categories or types of performance: economic, social,
and political. These are not mutually exclusive, however. For example, education could be viewed as an
index of political development to the extent that it
is a variable in political socialization, interest
articulation, and so forth. It is also a variable in
economic growth and development because improvement in
technical skill as well as overall educational capa-
bility may well determine, at least partially, how
much mobility and redistribution of wealth is likely
or possible in the social system. Examples can be
multiplied to show the interrelatedness of these categories.

Now to return to the vantage points. Since the
value of "unbiased" performance assessment is self-
evident, it is futile to belabor it. I shall return
later to this vantage point regarding the question of
the kind of data needed for so-called objective performance assessment. The other vantage points need
to be justified, however.

Vantage Point of the Citizenry

First, let me address myself to the vantage point
of the consumers of the policies of these regimes. It
can be argued that a favorable perception of performance, even when not supported by objective performance
data, will affect the response of the society to its
problems and the solutions to these problems. Such an
admittedly subjective perception by the citizenry—provided it is judiciously telescoped in time—could exude
enthusiasm that would positively affect the output of
the government and society. At the very least it will
prevent the acquisition of a fatalistic attitude,
which tends to be paralyzing. Furthermore, good performance rating by the citizenry may provide a requisite breathing space for carefully planned solutions
to exhibit their impact. Finally, in a situation
where the military leadership lacks experience and
does not have total confidence in its political capabilities, a good rating may offer invaluable assurance, which undoubtedly has an impact upon the policy
choices and policy formulation processes of the
leaders.

Consider the case of the United States economic
dilemma. The chairman of the National Economic Council went before a congressional committee in January
1975. He was asked what he thought about a proposed
tax cut and rebate. His answer, surprisingly, demon-
strates my point. He was not optimistic that by itself such a program could have any significant effect
on the economy. The value of such a measure, in his
judgment, was its possible psychological effect on
Americans. The economist thus admitted that in such
a case citizens' perception, not objective performance, is the determinant variable.

Of course the argument is not that high economic
performance, or any other type of performance, can
continue to exist for long simply because people think
it exists. The penalty for an ultimate failure to
convert a favorable subjective performance to high
objective performance can be extremely costly to the
leadership, and it may be most crushing and devastating in its impact on the society at large.

How does one get at these subjective perceptions
of the citizenry? One tool is the analysis of newspapers, particularly of letters to the editor, editorial opinion, and pronouncements from "significant"
sections of society (including students, labor, etc.).
There are some disadvantages to using this tool.
Since in many societies less than 30 percent of the
citizenry is literate, the views of the nonliterate
majority are not necessarily included. Nor is it sufficient to argue that the literate probably represent
the nonliterate because they are held in high esteem
for possessing the gift of the written word. Put
simply, we are no longer certain that the pen is
"mightier than the sword." In addition, freedom of
expression in a military regime is often severely
restrained. Consequently one could argue that it is
unlikely that literate people would care to write letters critical of the government. Nor can we be sure
that editors are free to publish such letters. It may
well be a situation of publish and be damned. But it
is extremely significant if, despite the constraints
on freedom of the press, decidedly critical opinions
of the regime emerge in the country's press.

While the question of the freedom of the press
in a military regime is an empirical one, just as it
is in civilian regimes, there remains the fact that
the opinions of a large portion of the society may be
left untapped. We therefore need to supplement this
method with formal and informal questionnaires. These
provide a qualitative and quantitative measurement of
the citizen's perception of the performance of the
military regime. Whether or not the citizen is literate need not be a problem here.[5] Specifically, such a
questionnaire might include questions of the following
sort:

1. How much economic growth do you think has
    occurred during the military rule?

2. How much equity of economic development
    have you seen during this period?

3. How much social development has occurred,
    in your perception, during military rule?

4. How much political stability have you seen?

5. How much unity or disunity has occurred in the country?

6. How much do you feel a participant in the political system?

7. Do you feel that your interests are sufficiently represented?

8. How much freedom do you feel exists?

9. On the whole, using whatever yardstick you wish, has military rule been more satisfactory than civilian rule?

We must recognize that the citizen may use an entirely different yardstick to measure performance. It may well be, for example, that he is unconcerned about the absence of democratic paraphernalia as long as he feels that his interests are somehow represented. Economic considerations may have preeminence.

The Military Regime Perspective

It seems reasonable to assume that in the choice and modification of strategy a good general not only will undertake to study the moves, capabilities, intentions, and attitude of the adversary but also must be cognizant of the mood, morale, attitude, and capabilities of his own troops. He must know what he has accomplished and what he needs to accomplish because these too may affect his decision. Since all these considerations involve interpretation, the general's point of view and perceptions are obviously crucial. This analogy applies to the military rulers and their vantage point. We need to ask them the following questions:

1. How much do they think they have promised?

2. How much do they think has been accomplished during their rule?

3. What do they judge their level of support to be?

4. What reasons do they adduce for their
   failures and successes?

5. How much do they think has to be done?

6. What do they think is needed in order to
   do what must be done?

How does one get these data? We can examine government "progress reports." We can look at the military
rulers' budget statements. We can examine their
speeches and public utterances. And we can look at
the interviews they have granted.

There is a prevalent practice among military rulers to outline the economic aims and goals of the government in development plans or similar documents. In
some cases military regimes also have political char-
ters. Typically, sectoral goals are set; strategies
are sometimes outlined; specific goals are often laid
down in terms of growth and unemployment; philosophies
to govern the distribution of wealth and resources are
spelled out; and in some cases general philosophic
predispositions are stipulated or are extractable. An
objective way to measure performance is to see what
proportion of the specific goals and promises of the
government have been achieved.

It does not seem unfair to hold these governments
to their performance targets. Of course there is the
problem that an exclusive dependence on this as an
objective measurement may be misleading. For example,
one government may deliberately promise very little
while another promises too much. Thus it may be necessary to consider past performance of the system,
available resources, and so forth. To do this is not
to deny that it is possible to attain a level of performance higher than that which the analysis of one's
resources might suggest.

Another approach that is useful in assessing
objective performance is to view the allocation of
natural resources—to note shifts or maintenance of
the status quo in the pattern of allocation. In the
face of extreme constraints on the availability of
societal resources, this may be a useful and sensitive indicator of the relative political muscle of
various groups. Both the operational or ordinary
budget and the capital or development budget are

important, and it is necessary to compare these allocations or expenditures with those of the preceding
civilian regime.[6] The priorities established in resource allocation may be a correct indication of the
value of the ruling regime and may also represent the
military elite's perception of what is pragmatic.

A third way to measure the so-called objective
performance involves the use of economic, political,
and social indicators of development.[7] Here it is
necessary to recall the point about the interdepen-
dence of the various categories of development. As a
result of such overlap, I have elected to lump all
these together as indicators of development:

1. GNP per capita growth rate

2. Unemployment statistics

3. Inflation rate

4. GPD growth rate

5. Rural/urban investment and allocation

6. Income distribution or, in the absence of
   this data, the pay structures of the public
   and private sectors as well as educational
   investment designed to equip the unquali-
   fied citizen to participate and share in
   the economy

7. Improvement in human resources

8. Literacy rate

9. Effectiveness or improvement of finance
   institutions

10. Gross investment rate

11. Degree of national integration and sense
    of national unity

12. Extent of political participation

13. Degree of administrative efficiency

14. Strength of labor unions

15. Degree of centralization of power

Up to this point it would appear that what I am
advocating is a case study approach. I remain convinced that within the African cultural milieu what
we must do is intensify the case studies. So long as
data are gathered within a clearly defined framework,
the task of comparative analysis, which is partly a
major function of theory, is facilitated immensely.

My own reservation is that we have prematurely
embraced theories based upon assumptions and contentions that, in the African context, remain suspect at
best. Consider the case of the reference group theory
as it has been applied to the study of the military.[8]
In general this theory contends that identification
with a social group necessarily involves internaliza-
tion of the group's core values. Conceivably one can
even psychologically identify with a group in which
one does not hold formal membership. The point to
remember is that the group with which one psychologically identifies constitutes one's significant referent, while that is not necessarily the case with all
social groups in which one holds membership. Unfortunately the application of this rather useful theory
to the military has attributed omnipotent powers to
military socialization within colonial officer schools.
Four points are central to this variant of reference
group theory:

1. Military socialization of the officer corps
   of many of the new states produces reference group identification with officer
   corps of the ex-colonial power and "concom-
   itant commitments to its set of tradition,
   symbols and values."[9]

2. These identifications and commitments affect
   the officer corps in their relationship with
   civilian political authority.

3. They also affect the behavior of these officers as government leaders should they ac-
   cede to political power.

4. Military socialization is more effective
   than civilian socialization.

The alleged efficacy of military socialization

is suspect in view of the fact that the military officers who led the coups in Ghana, Uganda, and Nigeria
(to mention a few) were all indoctrinated in British
or American military academies with the notion of
civilian supremacy and of noninterference of the military in politics. More perplexing is the fact that
within the same countries military regimes exposed to
the same military socialization pursued policies that
were diametrically opposed to one another. Furthermore, the reasons given for military intervention were
sometimes curiously divergent. One regime intervened
to bring "tyranny to an end" and to return the country
to democracy. Another toppled a duly elected and democratic government because of the superiority of the
"principle of one man one bread [*sic*]."[10] With the
exception of the case of the leader of the National
Liberation Council (NLC), examples of African military
leaders who admit to or believe in the influence of
their colonial military training in policy formulation
are rare indeed.[11] Huntington was right when he observed: "Military aid and military training are by
themselves politically sterile. They neither encourage nor reduce the tendencies for military officers to
play a political role."[12]

To clarify my position, my criticisms do not
apply to reference group theory in general. Rather,
they deal with the variant of it that has been applied
to military/political studies. It is futile a priori
to determine military socialization to be superior and
thus to establish the military as the only significant
referent. Allegedly, identification with significant
civilian reference groups is broken down and replaced
through isolation from past reference and membership
groups, "isolating [the military officer] from sources
of social, psychological support from his previous
beliefs."[13] Inevitable questions threaten this application of the theory. Is resocialization of officers
possible? What happens to foreign-trained officers
once they are reimmersed, at least partially, into
old membership groups or other sources of social and
psychological support from their previous beliefs? In
short, do we deny the existence of cross pressures?[14]

Consider the case of Major General Hassan Katsina,
who is the son of the traditional ruler of Katsina,
the Emir of Katsina. During the Ironsi military
regime he was made military governor of the northern
region. Following the decision to break up the region

into states, the regime then appointed him chairman of
the Interim Services Commission. Later on he was
named chief of staff of the Nigerian Army. Currently
he is the deputy chief of staff of Supreme Military
Headquarters and the commissioner in charge of establishment and service matters in the Federal Military
Government. He has always served as a member of the
Supreme Military Council, the highest ruling body of
the military regime. In addition, Major General
Hassan received overseas training in the Royal Military Academy Sandhurst, MONS Officer Cadet School,
Staff College, and the Royal College of Defense Studies. Yet on November 20, 1974 it was announced that
this most senior military officer, and certainly one
of the most powerful members of the military regime,
had been appointed the "Ciroma of Katsina." This is
a traditional title that establishes him as heir
apparent to his father's throne. [15]

In an interview Hassan said, "If it is the wish
of God that I should be a traditional ruler, I will
become a full-fledged traditional ruler and succeed
my father." Katsina is an emirate in one of the
twelve states of Nigeria. In terms of prestige, glam-
our, and power it does not begin to compare with the
positions of deputy chief of staff of Supreme Headquarters and member of the Supreme Military Council.
General Hassan was quite forthright in explaining his
success as a functionary of the military regime:
"With the experience gained from watching my grand-
father and father administer their emirate, I have
been able to do likewise. My guiding principle is my
father's advice to me when I became a military governor." [16] What should be noted here is that the ultimate credit for this man's being a successful functionary in the military was due, according to him, to
traditional primordial socialization. The fact that
he is willing to take off his mufti for the turban of
a traditional emirate suggests that military socialization is far from omnipotent, as is assumed.

Finally, it will become obvious that the analysis
of the politics of military regimes studied here does
not in fact suggest the validation of this variant of
reference group. We might go further to say that a
cursory examination of the policies of the other
African military regimes such as those of Mobutu, Amin,
and Kerekou does not support this theory. Consider
the anti-British policies of Amin and the socialism of

Kerekou. This is not to say that there are no significant reference groups. The intensification of case
studies and the analysis of policies may ultimately
establish a hierarchy of significant referents if
there is one.

      Within the literature there is what might be
called the formal organizational school regarding military regimes.[17] This school maintains that as an
organization the military is characterized by centralization, discipline, hierarchy, communication, esprit
de corps. These characteristics are in turn attributed to the armed forces in developing countries, so
that they are presented as possessing ideological and
structural cohesion, internal discipline, a commonly
shared belief system of secular rationality, puritanic
asceticism, and patriotic nationalism, and a commitment to modernization and public service. In short,
the armed forces of developing countries by definition
must perform as positive agents of development and
modernization.

      The deficiencies of the formal organization
school have been discussed elsewhere.[18] It will suf-
fice to state here:

1. This school does not take sufficient cogni-
   zance of institutional mutation and modification, which we know definitely accompany
   the process of institutional transfer from
   the developed states to the developing ones.
   The argument here is not that such institutional mutations and modifications are dysfunctional to the social system.

2. It is by no means absolutely clear that the
   alleged characteristics of military organizations of developed countries are not
   ascribed. Indeed how puritanic are the military organizations of the developed countries?

3. Moreover, given the technological and skill
   differentiation of the military establishment of developed countries on the one hand
   and the essentially combative composition
   and paucity of skill differentiation in the

military organizations of the developing
nations on the other, it could be argued
that the qualitative distinction affects
the capacities and performance of these
military organizations in the various
societies.

4. It is very doubtful that the military
socialization of the armed forces in the
developing countries has accomplished the
kind of attitude transformations assumed
by this school. Consider the number of
flare-ups and disaffections in the American
military. One could add to this the political factionalism in the French army at the
end of the last and at the beginning of the
present century when clerical and anticleri-
cal officers and Republican and anti-Republi-
can officers were at loggerheads.

Thirdly, there is the Samuel Huntington school,
which in a sense could be regarded as the "mass political participation determinist" school. To Huntington,
organizational factors are extrinsic and essentially
irrelevant in the calculation of the political performance of military regimes. What is relevant,
broadly speaking, is the social and political condition of the society—specifically the degree of mass
participation prevalent in the social system. Thus
Huntington postulates: "In the world of the oligarchy,
the soldier is a radical, in the middle-class world,
he is a participant and arbiter; as the mass society
looms on the horizon, he becomes the conservative
guardian of the existing order." In essence the crucial factor is the military's orientation toward mass
political participation. He writes, "The extent to
which a political officer corps plays a conservative
or reform role in politics is a function of the expansion of political participation in the society."[19]

One unfortunate factor here is the presumption
that all military regimes and officers harbor an
essentially conservative dogma that prevents them
from reacting favorably to changes presumed necessary
for the operation of the political processes of mass
societies.[20] This assumption by itself is perhaps not
incontrovertible. In any case it is not certain how

many truly mass societies have existed. It *is* certain
that in the modern African setting no societies con-
form to the ideal construct of a mass society, nor are
any likely to do so in our generation. Thus, quite
apart from my reluctance to accept as true the alleged
conservative monolithic predisposition of the military,
the absence of existing or even incipient mass societies in modern Africa is a constraint on the central
utility of this model. This is not to deny the possible contribution of Professor Huntington's general
observations, which are appropriately acknowledged
where applicable.

CHAPTER TWO

Assessment of Development Performance
of the Nigerian Military Regime

The Federal Military Government (FMG) admitted that
current estimates of principal economic indicators
tended to diverge from plan forecasts because changes
in the level and structure of economic activity had
been more rapid than foreseen or anticipated in 1970.
The FMG pointed out that the "oil boom which has occurred since the end of the civil war has marked a
turning point in the pace and process of economic
development of this country."[1] An examination of
table 1 (page 17) clearly indicates the nature and
dimensions of these changes.

Of particular significance in assessing performance both from the military regime's vantage point and
objectively are the data on 1) gross domestic product
(GDP), 2) growth rate, 3) investment ratio, 4) capital
formation, 5) gross national savings, 6) savings ratio,
7) GNP as a percentage of GDP, 8) government recurrent
expenditure, 9) government recurrent revenue, 10) budget surplus, and 11) rate of inflation. It is obvious
from table 1 that the GDP has increased much more than
envisaged in the development plan. The FMG believes
the Nigerian economic growth to have been generally
impressive. In his 1974 Independence Day broadcast
General Gowon indicated that, even allowing for factors of inflation, the economy grew at an average
annual rate of about 10.2 percent.[2] Added to this is
the dramatic increase in the gross national savings
as well as in the savings ratio. It appears that
recurrent revenue is reasonably balanced with recurrent expenditure for 1971 through 1973. (Obviously
the FMG can be thankful for its oil revenue.)

The government's figure on the inflation rate,
however, betrays the plan's undue optimism with
regard to what had become a worldwide problem. On

TABLE 1

COMPARISON OF PLAN FORECAST WITH CURRENT ESTIMATES 1970-71, 1971-72 AND 1972-73

	1970-71			1971-72			1972-73		
	PLAN FIGURE	ACTUAL ESTIMATES	INCREASE/ DECREASE	PLAN FIGURE	CURRENT ESTIMATES	INCREASE/ DECREASE	PLAN FIGURE	CURRENT ESTIMATES	INCREASE/ DECREASE
Gross Domestic Product (₦m)	3,171.2	4,178.4	+679.8	3,371.8	4,928.2	+961.6	3,639.4	5,402.4	+1,065.6
Growth Rate	4.2	30.6	+4.9	6.3	17.9	+6.2	7.9	9.6	+0.7
Capital Formation	710.0	911.2	+210.2	798.0	1,172.6	+374.6	836.0	1,300.4	+464.4
Investment Ratio (%)	18.4	18.9	+.4	18.9	20.0	+1.1	18.2	20.2	+2.0
Traditional Exports (₦m)	403.6	374.2	-29.4	428.4	364.0	-64.4	435.6	242.2	-193.4
Oil Exports (₦m)	520.6	517.2	-3.4	659.0	980.4	+321.4	739.0	1,186.4	+447.4
Total Exports (₦m)	924.2	891.4	-32.8	1,160.0	1,344.4	+184.4	1,174.6	1,428.6	+254.0
Imports (₦m)	660.0	718.4	+58.4	725.8	1,059.4	+333.6	816.4	956.4	+140.0
Current Account Balance (₦m)	-69.2	-50.0	-19.2	-41.0	-229.4	-188.4	-71.8	-315.0	-243.2
Gross National Savings	328.4	861.2	536.4	387.0	943.2	556.0	341.4	985.4	+644.0
Saving Ratio	9.2	19.0	9.8	10.0	17.0	+7.0	8.2	16.7	+8.5
G.N.P. as Percentage of G.D.P.	92.3	93.8	+1.5	91.5	94.4	+2.9	91.0	91.3	+0.3
Government Recurrent Revenue	637.2	848.0	+210.8	794.4	1,414.9	+620.5	947.6	1,527.1	+579.5
Government Recurrent Expenditure	571.8	792.0	+225.2	643.0	882.2	+239.2	686.0	1,118.8	+432.8
Budget Surplus	65.4	51.0	-14.4	151.4	532.7	+381.3	261.6	408.3	+146.7
Rate of Inflation	1.5	6.0	+4.5	1.5	9.5	+8.0	1.5	3.0	+1.5

Source: Nigeria, Federal Ministry of Economic Development and Reconstruction, Central Planning Office, *Second National Development Plan 1970-74, Second Progress Report*, Lagos: May 1974, p. 11.

TABLE 2
COMPOSITE CONSUMER PRICE INDICES, LOWER INCOME GROUP
(1960 = 100)

Item	1969	1970	1971	1972	Per cent Change 1970	Per cent Change 1971	Per cent Change 1972
All Items	132.3	150.6	174.7	179.6	13.8	16.0	2.8
Accommodation	126.1	129.7	132.4	135.4	2.9	2.0	2.2
Clothing	148.4	160.6	166.8	167.3	8.2	3.8	3.0
Drinks	137.5	140.1	146.1	152.7	1.9	4.2	4.5
Food	133.9	164.4	211.4	216.6	23.5	28.5	2.4
Fuel and Light	132.5	144.9	161.6	178.3	9.4	11.5	10.3
Other Purchases	134.8	151.5	164.6	169.0	12.4	8.6	2.6
Other Services	121.3	125.7	127.0	130.6	3.6	1.0	2.8
Tobacco, Kolanuts	92.2	97.1	98.8	102.6	5.3	1.7	3.8
Transport	132.0	143.4	144.0	149.4	8.6	0.4	3.7

Source: *Second Progress Report*, Lagos: The Central Planning Office, Federal Ministry of Economic Development and Reconstruction, 1974; p. 21.

this issue table 2 is enlightening. (See page 18.)
It was estimated that the inflation rate would increase
by 12 percent in 1974.[3]   The government asserted:
"These indices must be regarded as highly fragmented
since they also fail to capture movement in the level
of intermediate and capital goods prices. However, by
the partial measure of selected urban consumer price
indices, prices rose by 6 percent in 1970-71, climbed
further by 9.5 percent in 1971-72. Thereafter, it
fell by 3 percent in 1972-73."[4]   In slowing down
inflation the government credits its imports and its
excise duties in 1972/73 and its restraints on deficit
financing following the end of the civil war.[5]   Of
considerable importance to the assessment of development performance is the government statement that "the
substantial increases in the level of Gross National
Savings are traceable to the growth in public savings."[6]

     Table 3 (page 21) shows the actual capital ex-
penditure of the government from 1970 to 1973 and its
proportion of the 1970-74 revised effective capital
program. Although the government claimed that the
table shows how far each regional government had progressed with its implementation of the revised program,
it warned against a literal interpretation of the figures. According to the progress report: "The size of
the effective programme of each government for the
period 1970-74 was based on the assumption uniformly
made for all governments that 30 percent of the nominal
programme would be underspent. It is clear from all
available information that this assumption does not
hold for the Mid-West where actual underspending is
likely to be much below the 30 percent assumed." Moreover, the government explained:

     The rate of inflation has been increasing
     rapidly in most developed countries, and
     this is being transmitted to us in the form
     of high import prices. Furthermore, the
     inadequate executive capacity in the con-
     struction industry coupled with an acute
     shortage of an essential input like cement,
     led in the last three years to a very high
     rate of inflation in the construction indus-
     try. In consequence of and in response to
     these developments, the original costs set
     out in the Plan document now bear very lit-
     tle relationship to revised estimated costs.

Price rises alone cannot explain all
increases.[7]

For these reasons, actual capital expenditure as a
proportion of the allocated capital program, is not a
precise and correct indicator of real performance.
Nor can one convincingly argue that actual capital
expenditure as a proportion of the revised effective
capital program is a correct indicator of performance.

Analysis of the government figures regarding its
actual distribution of public expenditure does not
indicate any very major sectoral deviation of actual
expenditure from revised plan estimates.* It is interesting, however, that the only shift of some significance is the increase in the actual proportion of
expenditure in the social sector from 26 percent to
27.9 percent. If this holds through the entire life
of the plan, it could be interpreted as an expression
of social concern and a modification of government
position so as to demonstrate a greater concern for
equity. Of course a deeper analysis of sectoral performance is necessary before one can make a categori-
cal statement in this respect. Examine the planned
public capital investment broken down into its sectoral components (table 5, pages 22-23). In the
tables that follow (tables 6, 7, and 8, pages 24-26)
the actual sectoral capital expenditures are noted by
year. The so-called performance ratio can be gleaned
from the last column of the tables.

Agriculture

The government's allocation to the agricultural
sector and the "performance ratio" contained in table
6 speak for themselves. It is necessary to say more
regarding the government's perception of its agricultural performance, however. According to the FMG:

1. It had assumed full responsibility for agricultural research.

2. It had involved itself in direct primary
   production under the so-called Special
   Agricultural Scheme, setting up food companies in the Mid-Western, Kwara, and
   East-Central states.

---

*See table 4, page 21.

TABLE 3
ACTUAL CAPITAL EXPENDITURE 1970-73
AS A PROPORTION OF
REVISED EFFECTIVE CAPITAL PROGRAM 1970-74

	REVISED EFFECTIVE CAPITAL PROGRAM 1970-1974 ₦ MILLION	ACTUAL CAPITAL EXPENDITURE 1970-1973 ₦ MILLION	RATIO COL. 3 AS PERCENTAGE OF COL. 2
(1)	(2)	(3)	(4)
Federal Government ..	1,464.2	702.8	48.0
Benue-Plateau	64.5	44.3	68.7
East-Central	92.0	30.9	33.6
Kano	93.4	81.8	87.6
Kwara	40.6	27.9	68.7
Lagos	132.6	49.9	37.6
Mid-Western	65.8	67.0	101.8
North-Central	72.0	45.9	63.8
North-Eastern	75.1	48.4	64.4
North-Western	70.3	44.3	63.0
Rivers	57.8	45.1	78.0
South-Eastern	61.1	49.4	80.9
Western	147.8	78.4	53.0
TOTAL, ALL GOV'TS ...	2,437.2	1,316.1	54.0

Source: *Second Progress Report*, p. 28.

TABLE 4
PERCENTAGE DISTRIBUTION OF PUBLIC EXPENDITURE

SECTOR	REVISED PLAN PROPORTIONS 1970-1974	ACTUAL PROPORTIONS 1970-1973
Economic	52.7	49.6
Social	26.0	27.9
Administrative	19.0	19.4
Financial Obligation	2.3	3.1
TOTAL	100%	100%

Source: *Second Progress Report*, p. 28.

TABLE 5
Planned Public Capital Investment, 1970-74 (Revised)

Sector	Total	Federal Government	All States	Benue-Plateau	East-Central
(1)	(2)	(3)	(4)	(5)	(6)
Economic					
1. Agriculture	242.529	69.866	172.663	8.527	20.321
2. Livestock, Forestry and Fishing	62.247	9.619	52.628	2.173	5.100
3. Mining	36.661	36.661	—	—	—
4. Industry	162.660	67.394	95.266	10.000	16.287
5. Commerce and Finance .	49.755	13.192	36.563	1.684	1.332
6. Fuel and Power	102.433	90.650	11.783	0.540	—
7. Transport	885.563	645.492	240.071	32.155	10.202
8. Communications	129.209	129.209	—	—	—
9. Resettlement and Rehabilitation	30.254	18.800	11.454	—	—
10. Sub-Total	1,701.311	1,080.883	620.428	55.079	53.242
Social					
11. Education	363.232	152.064	211.168	14.500	16.000
12. Health	138.756	37.690	101.066	3.003	14.000
13. Information	85.319	65.000	20.319	2.999	2.000
14. Labour and Social Welfare	45.089	16.058	29.031	1.449	1.194
15. Town and Country Planning	59.079	22.569	36.510	1.100	3.500
16. Water and Sewage ...	148.676	—	148.676	12.266	10.032
17. Sub-Total	840.151	293.381	546.770	35.317	46.726
18. General Administration .	266.581	137.630	128.951	16.497	8.502
19. Defense and Security ...	346.183	346.183	—	—	—
20. Sub-Total	612.764	483.813	128.951	16.497	8.502
Financial					
21. Financial Obligations ...	73.601	73.601	—	—	—
22. Sub-Total	73.601	73.601	—	—	—
23. Grand Total	3,227.827	1,931.678	1,296.149	106.893	108.470

Source: *Second Progress Report*, p. 107

Kano (7)	Kwara (8)	Lagos (9)	Mid-Western (10)	North-Central (11)	North-Eastern (12)	North-Western (13)	Rivers (14)	South-Eastern (15)	Western (16)
47.278	4.164	7.734	9.683	5.600	6.223	9.358	10.177	19.005	24.593
2.734	1.360	6.520	5.100	1.972	4.406	5.314	6.949	2.988	8.012
—	—	—	—	—	—	—	—	—	—
3.720	5.574	3.720	11.563	5.216	5.893	3.028	7.906	7.226	15.134
7.010	5.000	2.500	2.574	0.904	1.304	3.830	4.929	5.020	0.476
1.630	1.000	—	2.108	—	1.262	0.400	0.250	2.000	2.000
11.000	6.380	60.504	20.162	18.892	22.655	10.050	15.680	12.660	19.711
—	—	—	—	—	—	—	—	—	—
—	—	—	—	—	—	—	—	11.454	—
73.372	23.478	80.978	51.190	32.584	41.743	31.980	45.891	59.113	73.080
16.200	6.902	11.870	15.374	19.081	21.426	21.237	11.150	8.428	49.000
9.820	5.744	10.680	10.340	5.045	11.420	8.978	6.424	4.186	11.424
0.558	0.850	0.200	3.838	0.581	1.851	0.164	2.827	1.080	3.371
2.066	3.114	3.791	2.040	2.511	3.786	1.496	2.856	0.800	3.928
3.200	0.350	2.700	1.491	6.807	5.471	0.790	2.100	4.000	5.000
9.000	6.132	31.376	8.164	23.988	9.773	6.755	4.000	4.100	23.090
40.844	23.092	60.617	41.247	58.013	53.727	39.420	29.357	22.594	95.813
6.552	7.155	42.360	2.137	2.309	13.027	15.536	5.206	3.670	6.000
—	—	—	—	—	—	—	—	—	—
6.552	7.155	42.360	2.137	2.309	13.027	15.536	5.206	3.670	6.000
—	—	—	—	—	—	—	—	—	—
—	—	—	—	—	—	—	—	—	—
120.768	53.725	183.955	94.574	92.906	108.497	86.936	80.454	85.377	174.893

TABLE 6
SECTORAL PERFORMANCE: AGRICULTURE

₦ MILLION

GOVERNMENT	ORIGINAL PLANNED EXPENDITURE 1970-74	REVISED PLANNED EXPENDITURE 1970-74	ORIGINAL PLANNED EXPENDITURE 1970-73	ACTUAL CAPITAL EXPENDITURE			TOTAL ACTUAL EXPENDITURE 1970-73	TOTAL ACTUAL CAPITAL EXPENDITURE 1970-73 AS A PROPORTION OF TOTAL REVISED PLANNED EXPENDITURE 1970-74 PER CENT
				1970-71	1971-72	1972-73		
Federal	61.675	69.866	45.134	2.382	10.665	21.087	34.134	48.9
Benue-Plateau	5.856	8.527	4.482	0.977	1.660	2.603	5.240	61.5
East-Central	20.178	20.321	15.280	1.164	1.419	2.903	5.486	27.0
Kano	33.478	47.278	25.300	4.046	5.518	8.028	17.592	37.2
Kwara	4.668	4.164	3.722	0.121	0.569	1.126	1.815	50.2
Lagos	6.400	7.734	4.200	0.025	0.796	2.240	3.059	39.6
Mid-Western	8.630	9.683	6.236	1.089	1.652	1.552	4.293	44.3
North-Central	4.657	5.600	4.980	0.711	1.048	1.842	3.601	64.3
North-Eastern	6.436	6.223	6.242	0.454	1.558	1.456	3.467	55.7
North-Western	7.880	9.358	5.950	0.421	1.565	3.132	5.119	54.7
Rivers	8.534	10.177	6.066	0.535	0.715	1.528	2.778	27.3
South-Eastern	19.005	19.005	11.270	2.034	3.144	2.198	7.376	38.8
Western	24.312	24.593	19.586	2.860	2.950	4.173	9.983	40.6
TOTAL	211.709	242.529	158.448	16.819	33.259	53.868	103.946	42.9

Source: *Second Progress Report*, p. 54.

TABLE 7

Sectoral Performance—Livestock, Fisheries and Forestry

Government	Original Planned Expenditure 1970-74	Revised Planned Expenditure 1970-74	Original Planned Expenditure 1970-73	Actual Capital Expenditure			Total Actual Expenditure 1970-73	Total Actual Expenditure 1970-73: Total Revised Planned Expenditure 1970-74 (%)
				1970-71	1971-72	1972-73		
Federal	6.506	9.619	5.544	0.139	1.238	2.276	3.653	38.0
Benue-Plateau	1.778	2.173	1.554	0.982	0.393	0.301	1.676	37.8
East-Central	5.100	5.100	3.450	0.562	0.645	1.068	2.275	44.6
Kano	2.734	2.734	2.184	0.415	0.711	0.843	1.069	72.0
Kwara	1.291	1.360	1.102	0.025	0.205	0.554	0.784	57.7
Lagos	5.510	6.520	3.402	0.142	0.728	0.815	1.685	23.9
Mid-Western	4.382	5.100	3.524	0.425	0.696	1.278	2.399	47.0
North-Central	2.067	1.972	1.410	0.298	0.696	0.527	1.521	77.1
North-Eastern	4.545	4.406	3.620	0.656	0.729	0.941	2.326	52.8
North-Western	3.544	5.314	2.970	0.407	0.485	1.594	2.486	46.8
Rivers	4.218	6.949	2.588	0.245	3.228	0.305	3.778	54.4
South-Eastern	2.988	2.988	1.282	0.259	0.897	1.901	3.057	102.3
Western	7.163	8.012	6.112	1.190	1.870	1.507	4.567	57.0
TOTAL	51.826	62.247	38.742	5.745	12.521	13.910	32.176	51.7

Source: *Second Progress Report*, p. 57.

TABLE 8

SECTORAL PERFORMANCE—AGRICULTURE, LIVESTOCK, FISHERIES AND FORESTRY

GOVERNMENT	ORIGINAL PLANNED EXPENDITURE 1970-74	REVISED PLANNED EXPENDITURE 1970-74	ORIGINAL PLANNED EXPENDITURE 1970-73	ACTUAL CAPITAL EXPENDITURE			TOTAL ACTUAL EXPENDITURE 1970-73	TOTAL ACTUAL EXPENDITURE 1970-73: TOTAL REVISED PLANNED EXPENDITURE 1970-74 (%)
				1970-71	1971-72	1972-73		
Federal	68.181	79.485	50.678	2.521	11.903	23.363	37.787	47.5
Benue-Plateau	7.634	10.700	6.036	1.075	2.053	2.934	6.062	56.6
East-Central	25.278	25.422	18.730	1.726	2.064	3.971	7.761	30.5
Kano	35.212	50.212	27.484	4.460	6.230	8.871	19.561	39.0
Kwara	5.959	5.524	4.824	0.146	0.774	1.680	2.600	47.1
Lagos	11.910	14.254	7.602	0.167	1.524	3.055	4.746	33.3
Mid-Western	13.012	14.783	9.760	1.514	2.348	2.830	6.692	45.3
North-Central	n6.724	7.567	6.390	1.009	1.743	2.368	5.120	67.7
North-Eastern	10.981	10.629	9.862	1.110	2.287	2.397	5.794	54.5
North-Western	11.424	14.672	8.920	0.828	2.050	4.726	7.604	51.8
Rivers	12.752	17.126	8.654	0.780	3.943	1.833	6.556	38.3
South-Eastern	21.993	21.993	12.552	2.293	4.041	4.099	10.433	47.4
Western	31.475	32.605	25.698	4.050	4.820	5.680	14.550	44.6
TOTAL	262.535	304.972	197.190	21.679	45.780	67.807	135.266	44.4

Source: *Second Progress Report*, p. 58.

3. It had established Agricultural Development Authorities, the National Agricultural Council, the Nigerian Agricultural Bank, the National Agricultural Research Council, and meteorological services.

4. It had created and operated the Chad Basin and the Sokoto-Rima Valley Authorities to develop agriculture in these areas.

5. It had provided agricultural grants to the states in the amount of ₦24.93 million during the years 1970-73. According to federal authorities, "The short-fall of 36 percent could be explained by the inability of many states to sponsor agricultural projects which could attract Federal grants." As of 1973 the government had channeled ₦1.403 million out of ₦2.683 million in grants to institutes for research on food and tree crops, vegetables, fruits, and crops for local industries. [8]

Moreover, in some states (North-Western, Western, and Mid-Western) group farming was initiated and experienced respectable growth. The Mid-Western, Kwara, and East-Central states established Food Production Companies to grow food for commercial purposes. The governments stepped up their efforts to increase productivity per acre by providing the farmers with improved seeds and seedlings. [9]

The Kwara, Western, Eastern, Mid-Western, and River governments established small hiring units for tractors and other equipment. Other states, such as North-Central and Benue-Plateau, followed their example. Of course, as the FMG has noted, "the main constraint with regard to agricultural mechanization is the lack of skilled personnel to set up mechanized hiring units." [10] Extension agencies were being set up by the states to supply farmers with improved planting materials and livestock, fertilizers, and chemicals. These agencies were also responsible for providing formal training to farmers and extension agents. For further information on agricultural performance, tables 7 and 8, which deal with sectoral performance in the areas of agriculture, livestock, fisheries, and forestry, are enlightening.

TABLE 9
The Performance of Selected Major Agricultural Exports

	1965-66 1966	1967-68 1968	1968-69 1969	1969-70 1970	1970-71 1971	1971-72 1972	January to June 1973
COCOA BEANS							
Foreign Exchange Earnings in (₦m)	56.5	103.4	105.2	133.0	143.2	101.2	65.3
Output (in 000 tons)	185	238	189	224	302	254	—
Export (in 000 tons)	190	209	174	196	271	228	126.0
Realized Price in ₦ per ton	149	494.7	604.6	678.5	528.4	443.9	518
COCOA BUTTER AND OTHERS							
Quantity (in 000 tons)	—	21	21	18	17	19	11.6
Earnings in (₦m)	—	12.2	16.6	15.4	10.4	12.2	9.3
GROUNDNUTS							
Foreign Exchange Earnings in (₦m)	80.6	76.0	71.6	43.4	24.2	19.2	14.9
Output (in 000 tons)	993	1,074	1,249	1,272	1,556	1,720	—
Export (in 000 tons)	573.0	648	525	291	136	107	72.6
Realized Price in ₦ per ton	71.2	117.3	143	149.1	177.9	179.4	205
GROUNDNUT OIL AND CAKE							
EXPORTS							
Quantity (in 000 tons)	237.0	285	272	252	143	140	89.3
Earnings (in ₦m)	28.7	28.8	31.8	34.2	19.6	16.8	12.9
PALM KERNEL							
Foreign Exchange Earnings (in ₦m)	44.8	20.4	19.6	21.8	26.0	15.6	5.4
Output (in 000 tons)	—	na	na	na	na	na	na
Exports (Quantity) 000 tons	394	161	179	185	242	212	54.5
Realized Price in ₦ per ton	56.9	126.7	109.5	117.8	107.4	73.6	99.1

	1965-66 1966	1967-68 1968	1968-69 1969	1969-70 1970	1970-71 1971	1971-72 1972	January to June 1973
PALM KERNEL CAKE AND OIL EXPORTS							
Quantity (in 000 tons)	—	188	217	218	248	246	26.8
Earnings (in ₦m)	—	8.2	10.2	10.4	7.8	6.6	2.9
PALM OIL							
Foreign Exchange Earnings in (₦m)	21.8	0.2	0.8	1.2	3.4	0.2	—
Output (in 000 tons)	—	na	na	na	na	na	na
Exports (in 000 tons)	143	3	8	8	20	2	—
Realized Price in ₦ per ton	76.7	66.7	100.0	150.0	170.0	100.0	—
COTTON							
Foreign Exchange Earnings in (₦m)	10.4	6.6	6.8	13.2	11.3	0.6	2.8
Output (in 000 tons)	—	206	439	465	352	—	—
Exports (Raw) (in 000 tons)	14.9	14	14	28	22	1	4.8
Realized Price in ₦ per ton	351	465.2	478.4	471.6	500.0	600.0	593
COTTONSEED							
Foreign Exchange Earnings in (₦m)	1.9	1.8	2.0	.24	6.2	2.6	0.4
Output (in 000 tons)	na	na	na	na	na	na	na
Exports (000 tons)	66	29	43	97	98	63	—
Realized Price in ₦ per ton	28.4	62.0	46.5	43.3	63.3	41.3	62.6

Source: *Second Progress Report*, p. 15.

In his October 1, 1974 speech, the head of state,
discussing the agricultural performance of his regime,
argued that:

1. most of the farms and plantations abandoned
   during the civil war had been rehabilitated
   and brought back into production;

2. the government had intensified its extension
   service efforts and increased the supply of
   fertilizers and other requirements of farmers;

3. the government had spent ₦230 million of its
   capital expenditure (1970-74) on agriculture;

4. the government had reformed the marketing
   board system of the country;

5. producer prices of all agricultural produce
   had risen in several cases by about 100% in
   the previous two years;

6. the Agricultural Bank had been effectively
   established in 1973 and in the first year of
   of its existence had disbursed ₦10 million
   in loans to farmers and farmers' cooperatives;

7. various state governments had established
   food production companies. [11]

Table 9 (pages 28-29) outlines the specific performance of various agricultural exports. It must be conceded that in this area performance is mediocre. The
astonishing thing about government policy is the considerable emphasis placed on cash crops for export.
In view of the price behavior of agricultural commodities for domestic consumption, it would appear that
not enough emphasis had been placed on encouraging
domestic agricultural producers.

On the whole, the agricultural subsector grew by
only 3 percent in 1973/74. Nevertheless, the government remained optimistic about a significant upturn in
this sector of the economy. It appears that the FMG
hoped to stimulate and encourage farmer productivity
through seedling and fertilizer subsidies, while increasing direct state activities in agriculture.

TABLE 10
Sectoral Performance—Mining

	Original Plan Allocation 1970-74	Revised Plan Allocation 1970-74	Actual Capital Expenditure 1970-71	Actual Capital Expenditure 1971-72	Actual Capital Expenditure 1972-73	Total Actual Capital Expenditure 1970-73	Total Expenditure 1970-73 as a Proportion of Revised Plan Allocation 1970-74 %
1. Survey of Mineral Resources	272,000	738,000	25,582	42,436	111,314.40	179,332.40	24.3
2. Airborne Geological Survey	500,000	680,000	19,440	37,906	201,315.50	258,711.50	38.0
3. Government Participation in Mining Industry	3,000,000	3,000,000	—	—	243.75	243.75	0.0
4. Rehabilitation of Enugu Coal Mines	1,400,000	7,286,420	2,705,000	200,000	7,572,400.00	10,477,400.00	143.7
5. Petroleum Training Institute	—	2,490,000	—	—	129,656.33	129,656.33	5.4
6. Development of Okaba Coal Mine	—	886,000	—	—	200,000.00	200,000.00	22.6
7. Nigerian Mining Corporation	—	2,160,000	—	—	—	—	—
8. Consultancy Work on the Coal Industry	—	70,000	—	—	—	—	—
9. National Survey of Underground Water Resources	3,000	172,000	5,874	—	14,125.81	19,999.81	11.6
10. Liquefied Petroleum Gas	1,269,000	1,269,000	269,000	—	—	269,000.00	21.2
11. Liquefied Natural Gas	—	—	—	—	—	—	—
12. Second Oil Refinery	2,500,000	18,000,000	—	—	98,000.00	98,000.00	0.5
TOTAL	8,944,000	36,661,420	3,019,072	280,342	8,327,055.79	11,632,343.79	31.7

Source: *Second Progress Report*, p. 60.

Mining and Manufacturing

Writers of the *Second Progress Report* minced no words when they noted: "Whereas targets in the mining subsector can be said to have been overshot in some senses, the performance in the public segment of the manufacturing subsector is not remarkable." It is admitted that, "more than in any other sector, the records of financial disbursement give a wrong impression of actual achievement." Nevertheless, the conclusion is that in view of "poor technological know-how in this area, the delay in procuring foreign expertise, and the complicated nature of the projects," the achievement in the mining subsector was quite satisfactory. The government expected most of the projects to be completed by the end of the fourth year of the plan.[12] Precise data on sectoral performance in mining are contained in table 10. (See page 31.)

The data in table 11 (below) not only provide information on physical performance but also support the government's report that "the performance in the public segment of the manufacturing subsector is not remarkable." Relying on its performance ratio, however, was optimistic.

Among the reasons adduced for the slow progress in the manufacturing subsector are:

1. Difficulties in completing feasibility studies
2. Initial difficulties with funding
3. Scarcity of willing and competent technical partners
4. Changes in sectoral priorities
5. Infrastructural constraints and
6. Cancellation of a number of projects

TABLE 11

Year	Performance Ratio
1970-71	27.3
1971-72	21.7
1972-73	43.6

Source: *Second Progress Report*, p. 61.

The government gave this account of the progress of manufacturing projects:

Out of about 150 projects listed in the

manufacturing plan only 55 can be regarded
as basically new manufacturing projects.
The others are rehabilitation projects;
blanket cash disbursement projects like:
Investment in New Industries, Pre-Invest-
ment Studies and Feasibility Studies; cash
disbursement projects: Small Scale Industries Credit Schemes and grants for encour-
agement of cooperatives and statutory corporations; development of Industrial Estates,
etc. Although about 52 projects in the entire manufacturing plan can be said to have
been completed or at an advanced stage of
implementation, only three of the 55 basically new manufacturing projects have been
completed. These are Prospect Textiles (in
Kwara), Oil Seed Processing and Sokoto Tan-
nery (in North-Western state). It must be
noted, however, that a few of the projects
under Investment in New Industries qualify
as basically new manufacturing projects and
some of these--especially in the Mid-West--
have been completed. Several others, including mainly the Federal projects, are approaching the advanced stages of implementation.
But on about 45 projects, the report is
either no progress, or the project has been
abandoned because of non-viability. Most
of the remaining projects are only now
approaching the stage at which they normally
should have entered the Development Plan.[13] *

General Gowon's Independence Day speech[14] in
1974 accentuated the positive somewhat disproportion-
ately with regard to the manufacturing subsector,
although his perception of the mining subsector performance was rather accurate. The general believed
that in mining the government had established a solid
foundation on which future development schemes would
be based. Among the components of this foundation:

1. Establishment of the Nigerian National
   Oil Corporation on and off shore

2. The holding of majority shares in all
   foreign oil companies

3. Steps to insure acquisition of the
   technical know-how necessary to run

*See table 12, page 34.

TABLE 12
SECTORAL PERFORMANCES—INDUSTRY

✻

GOVERNMENT	ORIGINAL PLAN ALLOCATION 1970-74	REVISED PLAN ALLOCATION 1970-74	ACTUAL CAPITAL EXPENDITURE 1970-71	ACTUAL CAPITAL EXPENDITURE 1971-72	ACTUAL CAPITAL EXPENDITURE 1972-73	TOTAL ACTUAL CAPITAL EXPENDITURE 1970-73	TOTAL EXPENDITURE 1970-73 AS A PROPORTION OF REVISED PLAN ALLOCATION 1970-74 %
Federal	69,296,000	67,394,000	—	3,787,139	6,783,409	10,570,548	15.6
Benue-Plateau	10,000,000	10,000,000	109,180	1,443,330	1,207,660	2,760,170	27.5
East-Central	12,040,000	16,287,090	1,406,000	1,584,320	1,527,340	4,517,660	27.7
Kano	3,720,000	3,720,000	50,000	108,344	194,000	352,344	9.4
Kwara	5,311,600	5,573,600	410,000	254,600	2,041,110	2,705,710	48.5
Lagos	3,720,000	3,720,000	—	121,696	24,726	146,422	3.2
Mid-Western	8,712,000	11,562,724	3,586,000	1,880,376	1,623,476	7,089,852	61.3
North-Central	5,136,000	5,216,000	198,658	563,968	923,130	1,685,756	32.3
North-Eastern	8,062,000	5,893,073	5,556	400,600	286,072	692,228	11.7
North-Western	2,428,000	3,028,000	120,000	285,509	970,192	1,375,701	45.4
Rivers	6,646,000	7,906,000	40,000	410,000	299,000	749,000	9.5
South-Eastern	3,464,000	7,226,000	500,639	1,851,994	1,686,296	4,038,929	55.9
Western	15,134,000	15,134,000	1,192,998	232,893	1,186,582	2,612,473	17.2
TOTAL	153,669,600	162,660,487	7,619,031	12,924,769	18,752,993	39,296,793	24.2

Source: *Second Progress Report*, p. 62.

an oil industry: prospecting, production, refining, transportation, and
distribution

4. The setting up of a Nigerian Mining
   Corporation to identify, prove, and
   mine all solid materials with the exception of coal, for which there is a
   separate corporation

According to General Gowon, the Federal Military
Government was directly involved in two salt refineries at Ijoko and Sapele that had just gone into operation. Furthermore, the FMG had embarked upon car
assembly plants (Volkswagen, Peugeot) in Lagos and
Kaduna. Peugeots from the Lagos factory were already
on the road by March 14, 1975 according to the *Daily
Times*. A second oil refinery at Warri and the Kaduna
superphosphate fertilizer plant were under construction.

The creation and the functioning of the Nigerian
Bank for Commerce and Industry, the Agricultural Credit
Bank, and the Nigerian Enterprise Promulgation Decree
were ticked off by the head of state as part of his
regime's achievements. It was expected that by 1980
the iron and steel industry in Kwara would be in production. A petrol, chemical, and nitrogen fertilizer
complex was also planned. The government believed
that a major problem in this area at the beginning of
the second development plan was that of reconstructing
the industrial establishments damaged during the war.
But it claimed that "by the middle of the Second Plan
period practically all manufacturing concerns in this
category had been reactivated."[15] Cement factories
had been brought back into operation and were now being
expanded.

Finally, the Nigerian government approved the
establishment of a partnership with the overseas company of Anglo-Dutch Shell BP and Italian-American Agip
Phillips. This partnership (60-40) was to establish
two liquified gas projects in Bonny and Escravos. Each
project would produce 1,000 million cubic feet of gas
per day. The FMG would own 50 percent of the tanker
fleet used in the gas industry.[16]

It is appropriate to quote the closing words of
this government progress report on the state of
Nigerian economic performance. Judging by the report,

even the government was not quite ready to give itself
superior marks for performance. It remarked that the
rosy picture painted in its report was largely due to
the rapidly growing mining sector of the economy.
"This sector accounts for about half the growth rate
recorded, accounts for large increases in government
revenue, is responsible for the much improved foreign
exchange situation, and contributes substantially to
capital formation." The government was concerned that
traditional sectors such as agriculture have not done
as well. It accepted the fact that the growth recorded
in this sector was largely due to the recultivation of
large tracts of land in the war-affected area. It also
expressed the fear that because petroleum is a wasting
asset that will not flow indefinitely, aggregate overall economic performance figures were less comforting.
The report said: "There is an urgent need for a bold
approach to give a new lease of life to agriculture
while promoting industrial development. The long-run
growth of the economy will to a large extent depend on
what happens in these two sectors." Two urgent implementation problems had arisen by the time of the progress report: lack of executive capacity and lack of
familiarity of executive ministry officials with the
content of programs as outlined in the plan. In the
words of the report:

> It is appropriate to mention here that a
> number of implementation problems have come
> to light since the Plan was launched. Two
> of them are very important and deserve urgent
> attention. The first is that in some of the
> executive Ministries officials are not quite
> familiar with the content of their programmes
> under the Plan. This may be due to stall
> changes and shortages. It is the duty of
> every head of department and all his senior
> staff to take greater interest in, and be
> constantly informed of progress in the im-
> plementation of his Ministry's plan projects,
> whether these projects are being executed
> directly by the Ministry or on its behalf
> by a contractor or the Ministry of Works.
> Every official should always be ready to dis-
> cuss his Ministry's projects with confidence.
> Secondly it has become evident that in many
> areas executive capacity is still a big prob-
> lem. There is a shortage of technical staff
> to conduct initial studies and carry out the

necessary preparatory work without which
projects cannot be implemented even when
funds are available. Complaints about
shortage of funds are, quite often, not
real. The real bottleneck is inability to
prepare projects. There are of course instances in which financial constraints have
held back the implementation of plan
projects.[17]

Nevertheless, the government believed that generally
the country had made fairly good progress under the
plan. This optimism is significant because of our
interest in the government's image of its own performance.

Education

One of the most important decisions of the government in the area of education is the proposed Universal Primary Education (UPE) in Nigeria. Although
this would take effect in 1976, in 1974 steps had
already been taken and expenditures incurred in prep-
aration for this important government policy. The
federal commissioner of education referred to Universal Primary Education as an "educational revolution."
A total of 46,000 student teachers started training
for the project, and all existing 150 teacher-training
institutes had been expanded. The trainees were given
free tuition, boarding facilities, and allowances.
The government also established a National Teaching
Service to ensure comparable service conditions between
teachers and other public servants. Teacher trainers
were recruited from overseas countries.[18]

Typical of the changes in education after the
military took over are those detailed in the following
report in the North-Eastern State.

To cope with the UPE programme three new
teachers' colleges will be opened this month
by the North Eastern State Ministry of Education which has earmarked ₦163.7 m. as capital and recurrent expenditure for its 1974-
1980 development plan. The plan includes the
building and expansion of primary schools,
teachers colleges, and turning secondary
schools into comprehensive secondary schools.

There are at present 770 primary schools in
the State whose provisional population figure exceeds 15m. About 1,942 additional
classrooms will be opened during the 1974-
75 financial year. Before the creation of
new states there were 19 secondary schools
in the North Eastern State but now there a
are 43. Expansion has already started at
10 secondary schools to enable them to accom-
modate 1000 student teachers each. Four
craft-trade schools have been merged with
secondary schools to form comprehensive secondary schools.[19]

The FMG amended the Nigerian constitution to
transfer higher education from the "Concurrent Legislative List" to the "Exclusive Federal List." Other
levels of education were transferred to the "Concurrent Legislative List."[20] The 1970-74 revised federal
allocation for capital expenditure on education was an
approximately ₦360 million. The total enrollment in
primary schools rose from 3.5 million in 1970 to 4.5
million in 1973—a growth of nearly 30 percent in three
years without a UPE program.[21] Federal government colleges for boys increased by 300 percent from four to
twelve, during the military regime's rule. Federal
government colleges for girls experienced a 600 percent
growth, from two to twelve. Federal Schools of Sci-
ences and Arts were opened at Sokoto, Mubi, and Ogoja,
and the Federal Science School moved to its permanent
site. Four new colleges of technology and nine trade
centers were established by the state governments.
University enrollment rose from under 10,000 to 20,000
in 1975. Even more dramatic was the plan of the
University of Lagos to take in 10,000 students in 1975
alone—almost double the student enrollment at the
University of Ibadan prior to the military regime. The
number of Nigerian medical schools had also increased
from two to five during military rule.[22]

The government was severely criticized in some
quarters, however, for not introducing free secondary
education. Some even believe that the government had
the resources to introduce free university education.
This will be discussed later in the chapter.*

---

*See table 13, page 39.

TABLE 13
Sectoral Performance: Education

Government	Original Plan Allocation 1970-74	Revised Plan Allocation 1970-74	Actual Capital Expenditure 1970-71	Actual Capital Expenditure 1971-72	Actual Capital Expenditure 1972-73	Total Actual Expenditure 1970-73	Total Actual Expenditure 1970-73 as a Proportion of Revised Plan Allocation 1970-74 %
Federal	98,244,000	152,064,370	1,662,915	35,215,045	32,192,474	69,070,434	45.4
Benue-Plateau	10,490,000	14,500,000	926,560	1,854,850	2,650,000	5,431,410	37.4
East-Central	16,000,000	16,000,000	686,620	3,110,662	1,392,550	5,189,832	32.4
Kano	16,200,000	16,200,000	2,225,010	3,306,110	4,447,600	9,978,720	61.5
Kwara	5,216,800	6,902,240	805,100	1,259,885	2,474,675	4,539,660	65.8
Lagos	7,618,000	11,869,970	1,006,316	1,294,302	878,567	3,179,185	26.8
Mid-Western	13,526,000	15,375,000	2,544,169	3,234,818	3,352,130	9,131,117	59.4
North-Central	18,284,000	19,080,760	1,692,250	5,012,630	8,853,300	15,558,180	81.5
North-Eastern	13,021,720	21,425,881	1,107,458	3,094,736	4,508,069	8,710,263	40.6
North-Western	14,830,000	21,237,000	2,527,000	4,492,000	4,716,000	11,735,000	56.2
Rivers	11,150,000	11,150,000	891,742	2,565,542	2,258,040	5,715,324	51.2
South-Eastern	8,428,000	8,428,000	300,000	376,672	2,281,894	2,958,566	35.1
Western	49,000,000	49,000,000	4,871,200	2,939,132	5,229,119	13,039,451	26.6
Total	282,007,720	363,232,221	21,246,340	67,756,384	75,234,418	164,237,142	45.2

Source: *Second Progress Report*, p. 85.

TABLE 14
SECTORAL PERFORMANCE—TRANSPORT SUMMARY TABLE

PROJECTS	ORIGINAL PLAN ALLOCATION 1970-74 (₦)	REVISED PLAN ALLOCATION 1970-74 (₦)	ACTUAL CAPITAL EXPENDITURE 1970-71 (₦)	ACTUAL CAPITAL EXPENDITURE 1971-72 (₦)	ACTUAL CAPITAL EXPENDITURE 1972-73 (₦)	TOTAL ACTUAL CAPITAL EXPENDITURE 1970-73 (₦)	TOTAL EXPENDITURE 1970-73 AS A PROPORTION OF REVISED PLAN ALLOCATION 1970-74 (%)
FEDERAL PROGRAMS	335,566,000	645,492,494	35,118,377	55,456,588	96,578,520	187,153,485	29.0
(a) Roads and Bridges	192,416,000	398,884,320	23,004,238	41,018,570	74,367,753	138,390,561	34.7
(b) Railway	43,676,000	80,756,654	11,489,840	4,184,736	12,946,636	28,621,212	23.1
(c) Civil Aviation	27,600,000	49,736,000	617,562	2,515,164	925,182	4,057,908	8.2
(d) Airways	23,684,000	61,564,000	6,737	2,441,146	5,381,289	7,829,172	12.7
(e) Inland Waterways	5,414,000	9,132,520	—	120,972	1,043,660	1,164,632	12.8
(f) Maritime Services	510,000	1,253,000	—	28,000	969,000	997,000	80.0
(g) Shipping	6,300,000	6,700,000	—	—	180,000	180,000	2.7
(h) Ports	35,966,000	37,466,000	—	5,148,000	765,000	5,913,000	15.8
STATES PROGRAMS	154,312,000	240,070,883	22,258,545	31,021,621	71,930,007	125,210,173	52.1
1. Benue-Plateau (a) Roads	13,980,000	32,011,080	4,702,400	4,860,400	8,057,510	17,620,310	55.0
(b) Waterways	40,000	144,000	—	—	96,000	96,000	66.6
2. East-Central—Roads	10,002,000	10,202,000	—	1,450,057	668,017	2,118,074	20.7
3. Kano—Roads	11,000,000	11,000,000	2,098,902	2,972,468	6,316,756	11,388,126	103.5
4. Kwara—Roads	6,700,000	6,380,000	391,000	170,000	1,298,500	1,859,500	29.1
5. Lagos—Roads	8,000,000	60,504,400	1,644,118	3,262,220	19,801,410	24,707,748	40.8
6. Mid-West—(a) Roads	17,782,000	20,002,000	2,008,000	5,850,000	7,973,426	15,831,426	79.0
(b) Waterways	140,000	160,000	—	—	—	—	—
7. North-Central—Roads	12,642,000	18,891,462	847,910	603,894	2,720,358	4,172,162	22.1
8. North-Eastern—Roads	19,940,000	22,655,143	4,425,340	3,294,368	5,124,281	12,843,989	56.7
9. North-Western—Roads	6,620,000	10,050,000	267,168	594,025	3,268,660	4,129,853	41.1
10. Rivers—(a) Roads	10,980,000	11,680,000	495,828	2,720,322	10,242,491	13,458,641	115.1
(b) Waterways and Air	4,000,000	4,000,000	581,702	1,260,000	1,106,226	2,947,928	73.7
11. South-Eastern—(a) Roads	10,400,000	10,440,000	50,008	1,258,300	2,943,437	4,251,745	40.7
(b) Waterways	2,220,000	2,220,000	155,923	82,777	414,426	653,126	29.4
12. Western—Roads	16,826,000	19,710,798	4,590,246	2,642,790	1,898,509	9,131,545	46.3
GRAND TOTAL	486,838,000	885,563,377	57,376,922	86,478,209	168,508,527	312,363,658	35.3

Source: *Second Progress Report*, p. 71.

Transport

In his 1974 report to the nation the head of state claimed that:

1. the Federal Military Government had reconstructed about 2,200 miles of roads and
was still working on a total of 1,600 miles;

2. Enugu Airport had been reconstructed and
contracts had been awarded for the expansion of the Lagos, Jos, and Calabar airports;

3. the Nigerian Port Authority had completed
the rehabilitation of war-damaged port facilities in Calabar and Port Harcourt, and attempts at the modernization of the Nigerian
Railways were being intensified;

4. the FMG would have spent about ₦630 million
on transport by March 31, 1975.[23]

Of notable importance was the government decision to
take over trunk "B" roads, which had been the domain
of the state governments. This move would free the
state governments to concentrate on feeder roads of
significance to agricultural production and distribution.*

Labor

The federal and state governments grew considerably during the plan period. For example, in 1972 the
Federal Civil Service had an 8 percent growth in wages
paid while the State Civil Services had a 15 percent
growth. The increasing role of the government in the
plan accounts for this growth. In the same year,
federal government and quasi-government corporations
and companies experienced a wage growth of 11 percent.
In state government-directed companies and corporations wages rose by 18 percent.

The progress report, however, was blunt in warning that this encouraging wage growth should not divert
attention from the "massive employment problem posed

---

*See table 14, page 40.

by the planned expansion in the outflow of young,
literate men and women from the various institutions."
In a more positive vein the report pointed out that
"the development of small-scale industries was the most
promising direction in which to look for a major contribution towards job creation, and although the pace
of job creation during the first phase of the Plan has
probably declined somewhat in tempo, it is encouraging
to note that employment indices confirm that expansion
is taking place amongst small-scale concerns. Manpower policy will continue to lay emphasis on expansion in this area."[24]

In addition to increasing the various institutions
of higher learning and secondary and primary schools,
the federal government sought to improve the country's
management capabilities through the creation of the
Nigerian Council for Management Education and Training, with the Center for Management Development as its
operational arm. One of the notable undertakings of
the center has been its organization of seminars, lectures, and workshops aimed at explaining the revalua-
tion and purchase of businesses under the Nigerian
Enterprise Decree. It has researched and sponsored
lectures, workshops, and seminars dealing with management practices and training. The consulting branch of
the center was established to advise and counsel
Nigerian businessmen who want to know how to operate
small and medium enterprises.

In accordance with the Industrial Training Fund
Decree No. 37 of 1971, certain employers were expected
to contribute funds to the Industrial Training Fund to
enable it to organize various skill-training programs.
This fund was used to reimburse expenditures of students in training or on attachment programs.[25] Finally,
a Federal Administrative Staff College went into operation in 1974. (See table 15, page 43.)

A different appraisal of government's effort in
the labor field is expressed by Professor B. J. Dudley.
Estimating the number of unemployed and underemployed
to be 5.3 million, he argues that unemployment was
increasing and that the ranks of the unemployed now
included people of all ages, educational levels, and
professional skills. He suggests that neither the
civilian government (1962-68) nor the military regime
(1970-74) took employment as a primary objective, for
neither the development plan of the civilian regime

TABLE 15

SECTORAL PERFORMANCE: LABOUR AND SOCIAL WELFARE

₦

GOVERNMENT	ORIGINAL PLAN ALLOCATION 1970-74	REVISED PLAN ALLOCATION 1970-74	ACTUAL CAPITAL EXPENDITURE 1970-71	ACTUAL CAPITAL EXPENDITURE 1971-72	ACTUAL CAPITAL EXPENDITURE 1972-73	TOTAL ACTUAL EXPENDITURE 1970-73	TOTAL ACTUAL CAPITAL EXPENDITURE 1970-73 AS A PROPORTION OF REVISED PLAN ALLOCATION 1970-74 %
Federal	6,088,000	16,058,060	642,080	1,958,748	8,194,056	10,794,884	66.0
Benue-Plateau	450,000	1,448,930	31,000	147,690	87,270	265,960	18.0
East-Central	1,000,000	1,194,000	—	231,837	202,100	433,937	22.0
Kano	2,066,000	2,066,000	60,148	35,572	372,867	468,587	22.6
Kwara	2,664,000	3,114,000	1,025,000	803,000	836,000	2,664,000	85.0
Lagos	1,800,000	3,791,000	15,046	141,828	145,042	301,916	7.0
Mid-Western	752,000	2,040,000	91,084	79,224	13,841	184,149	10.0
North-Central	1,928,000	2,511,315	64,070	267,798	110,686	442,554	17.0
North-Eastern	1,750,200	3,785,526	747,194	891,343	619,378	2,257,915	59.6
North-Western	1,480,000	1,496,000	44,074	89,250	160,288	293,612	19.0
Rivers	836,000	2,856,000	100,000	160,000	2,088,095	2,348,095	82.0
South-Eastern	800,000	800,000	386,151	96,489	72,087	554,727	69.3
Western	3,928,300	3,928,300	409,016	317,150	583,027	1,309,193	33.3
TOTAL	25,542,500	45,089,131	3,614,863	5,219,929	13,484,737	22,319,529	49.5

Source: *Second Progress Report*, p. 98.

nor that of the Gowon military regime stressed it.
Portions of Dudley's article are quoted at length in
the note because it represents a different performance
perception and carries in it ominous predictions and
warnings.[26]

Equity and Social Justice

Two of the three declared principal goals of government fiscal policy were: 1) "to minimize existing
inequities in wealth, income and consumption standards
which may tend to undermine production efficiency,
offend a sense of social justice and endanger political
stability" and 2) "to maintain reasonable economic and
price stability in the face of inherent inflationary
pressure.[27]   These are in line with the government's
five principal objectives:

1. A unified, strong, and self-reliant nation

2. A great and dynamic economy

3. A just and equalitarian society

4. A land full of equal opportunities for
   all its citizens

5. A free and democratic society [28]

Points 3 and 4 call for policies committed to the
realization of equity or economic development, not
just economic growth. Similarly, the declared principal goals of fiscal policy move in the direction of
sharing of economic wealth. Now let us focus on how
the government and others see governmental performance
in this respect.

Judging from the fiscal policy goal quoted above,
the government considered price stabilization one
instrument for attaining social justice.   Toward that
end the government used a

> wage freeze (the post-Adebo freeze),
>
> import liberalization (discussed earlier)
>
> price control mechanisms through the crea-
> tion of the Price Control Board (as well
> as the National Supply Company),

     rent control, and

     surplus budgeting.

The government concluded that "the combined instruments [wage freeze and price control] seemed to have
worked during 1972, but since 1973, the price push
seems to have been on the increase once more, this
time partly as a result of the devaluation of the
naira in February and partly as a result of shortfalls
in the domestic production of certain items of food
stuff."[29] It conceded that the price of livestock
feed as well as the resulting increases in the prices
of eggs and chickens was problematic. Although the
general price index rose by 17 percent in 1971 and
then suddenly dropped to about 3 percent by 1972, in
1973 the estimated rise was nearly 12 percent. Thus,
between 1970 and 1974 an average rise of about 7 percent per annum can be presumed. The government report
noted that by ordinary standards this was quite high.

     All in all, at the time of the *Second Progress
Report* the government judged its objective of minimiz-
ing existing inequalities in wealth, income, and consumption standards to have been somewhat elusive.

> Measures have been taken to control rents in
> urban centres, and to raise the income of
> farmers producing traditional export crops.
> Surely these do not get to the root of the
> problem. One approach is to determine an
> optimal distribution of national product
> between labour incomes and rents and profits,
> and within labour incomes, to ensure an equit-
> able allocation between low income and high
> income earners. As much as these dimensions
> are concerned, not much has been done.[30]

After the publication of this report, however, the
Gowon government received and accepted the report of
the Udoji Commission.[31] The government believed that
the new wage policy (a la Udoji) would reduce dispari-
ties between earnings in the public and private sectors on the one hand and between the low and high
income workers within each sector on the other. Let
us compare the old and new wage structures.

     The new wage structure narrowed the gap between
the highest paid and the lowest paid in each service.
In the universities the salaries of the professors and

TABLE 16

RANK	OLD SCALE SALARY	UDOJI SCALE SALARY
Professor	6,600	8,730-11,025 9,819-12,411
Lecturer II	2,760-3,660	5,350-6,430
Permanent Secretary	6,480-6,960	11,577-13,959
Lowest-Paid Worker	312	720-870

Source: *Daily Times,* December 28, 1974.

TABLE 17
RANGE OF BENEFITS FROM UDOJI AWARDS

SALARY GROUP	OLD GRADES ₦		NEW SALARY GRADES ₦	
	MIN	MAX	MIN	MAX
1	312	612	720	870
2	336	878	800	980
3	336	1,016	900	1,280
4	406	1,950	1,100	1,380
5	492	2,040	1,370	1,810
6	516	2,592	1,630	2,310
7	848	2,688	2,000	3,000
8	482	2,988	2,780	3,980
9	3,090	4,140	3,980	5,340
10	3,900	4,140	5,350	6,430
11 [Sm 1]	5,064	5,472	5,445	6,905
12 [Sm 2]	—	—	6,129	7,749
13 [Sm 3]	5,064	6,480	6,895	8,730
14 [Sm 4]	5,472	7,320	7,760	9,810
15 [Sm 5]	6,240	6,480	8,730	11,025
16 [Sm 6]	6,480	6,961	9,819	12,411
17 [Sm 7]	6,480	7,860	11,043	13,959

Source: *Daily Times,* December 28, 1974, pp. 10, 11, 12.

lecturers were closer, with the lecturer grade II
starting at ₦5,350-6,430. (See table 16, page 46.)
In the Nigerian civil service, where most permanent
secretaries used to be placed in groups 3 and 4 (₦6,960
and ₦6,480), permanent secretaries were now put on Sm 6
(₦11,577-₦12,411) and in exceptional cases on SM 7
(₦12,015-₦13,959). The messenger (lowest-paid worker)
moved from ₦312 to ₦720. (See table 17, page 46.)

   In terms of entry points the lowest-paid worker
now earned 6.21 percent of the salary of the administrative head of the ministry instead of 4.81 percent.
Although this ratio is still not satisfactory relative
to the public-sector wage structure in the developed
world, it represents an improvement. Similarly, whereas
under the old pay structure a lecturer received 41.81
percent of a professor's salary in terms of entry
points, under the new plan the lecturer received 61.27
percent. Moreover, the discrepancy between the public
and private sectors was significantly narrowed, if not
completely eliminated. Finally, the establishment of
a National Teaching Council and a National Unified Wage
Structure eliminated the discriminatory wages and conditions of service that in the past made teaching a
less attractive career to ambitious young college
graduates.

   The pension and gratuity were also adjusted. Of
course government's good intentions do not always
materialize. The Udoji Commission gave rise to more
than 750 petitions in the space of one month. According to the *Daily Times*, "Most of these petitions have
come from trade union organizations, federal and state
civil services, government corporations, universities,
and technical institutions. More are still expected
this week."[32]

   The military regime seemed bewildered by the tre-
mendous number of industrial actions (strikes, etc.)
that greeted the Udoji award. These actions led
General Gowon to declare that it is "unjust" and
unfair for people not to show appreciation for the
government's efforts at improvement.

   The honest attempts of government to better
   the lot of its workers are being deliberately
   misinterpreted and efforts have been made to
   whip up the feelings of one sector of the public service against the other. . . . there is

> a limit to what any responsible government
> can tolerate in the face of calculated plan
> to disrupt the orderly progress of our
> nation.[33]

The truth of the matter is that despite the government's guarantee that prices would be controlled at
pre-Udoji award levels there were changes in commodity
prices, as illustrated in table 18. (See page 49.)
Compared with price increases in luxury goods, the
rise in food prices seems modest. The economic editor
of the *Daily Times* aptly observed that this was because

> workers did not spend their arrears so much
> on food or fish. So the demand for food items
> remained stable at pre-Udoji level. One could
> have expected no increase at all in the prices
> of foodstuff. But the sellers, middlemen--not
> the producers themselves--cashed in on the in-
> creased spending power of the workers. They
> succeeded. For I recalled that a messenger
> in one of the ministries bluntly told a retailer
> that money is no longer his problem. It's
> true; there was cash to throw around. But as
> we shall soon see workers have less than three
> months to return to square one! The major
> items of expenditure during the one week be-
> ginning from January 17 were furniture and
> electrical appliances. Nothing less than an
> estimated 75 per cent of the workers' arrears
> went on these items. A medium-sized refrig-
> erator, which before Udoji was sold at ₦180,
> now costs ₦225--a 25 per cent increase. The
> price of an electric fan went up from ₦86.00
> to ₦120.00, an almost 40 per cent increase.
> Unfortunately, there were not enough for the
> money which the worker held. Within one week,
> the department stores and the small electri-
> cal stores in Lagos made sales which they
> could not have made in three months.[34]

Voluntary agencies in Kwara increased their secondary
school fees by 60 percent, and other states followed.
The Western government took over the control of post-
secondary educational institutions in a bid to prevent
further rises.[35]

> The point is not that government attempts to nar-
row wages were a complete success. Nor is the argument

TABLE 18
CHANGES IN COMMODITY PRICES

BEFORE UDOJI		AFTER UDOJI	% RISE
Refrigerator	₦180	₦225	25.0
Electric fan	₦ 86	₦120	39.5
Stereo Amplifier	₦205	₦235	14.6
Radio cassette	₦ 60	₦ 84	40.0
Electric cooker	₦120	₦140	16.7
Vono mattress	₦ 34	₦ 38	11.8
Vono pillow	₦ 1	₦ 1.50	50.0
Cushioned chair	₦250	₦ 3	25.0
Coolers	₦340	₦371	9.1
Electric iron	₦ 14	₦ 17.50	25.0
Transportation			
Mini-bus fare			
(Yaba to Surulere)	5k	10k	50.0
(Lagos-Palm Grove)	10k	10k	—
Clothing materials—No appreciable increases observed.			
Food Items			
Packet of sugar	50k	55-60k	10-20
Tin of milk	10k	10k	—
Beef per pound	55k	80k	45.5
Tinned tomatoes	12k	15k	25.0
Drinks			
Fanta	10k	12k	20.0
Coca Cola	10k	12k	20.0
Star Beer	40k	55k	37.5
Heineken	55k	65k	18.2
Big Stout	50k	55k	10.0

An increase of 15-20% was recorded for all food ingredients while the prices of assorted fish went up by 30%.

Source: *Daily Times,* February 8, 1975.

about the merit or lack of merit in the Udoji recommendations or the government white paper on the recommendations per se. But there does appear to have been
a conscientious attempt on the part of the government
to spread some of the benefits of economic growth. As
in the case of the Indigenisation Decree, which will
be discussed later, the new wages had some unanticipated results.

Critics, among them Chief H. O. Davies and Tai
Solarin, argued that a more effective way to spread
the benefit of economic growth would be for the government to assume, as in Kuwait, the full burden of
secondary education and health services for all its
citizens. In their judgment, the increase in oil
revenue, a consequence of a 300 percent price increase
and increased production, made this possible. Chief
Davies suggested that the Nigerian government should:

1. give private individuals either total abolition or a drastic reduction in income
   tax and custom duties on essential goods;

2. initiate subsidy schemes and ensure that
   farmers obtain world market prices for
   their products;

3. reduce taxes on profits of businesses to
   enable companies to pay the Udoji awards;

4. come to the aid of "hard-pressed poor parents" by taking over all elementary and
   secondary schools and offering free education and medical services for all.

He concluded: "In all seriousness, it is wrong for an
affluent society to permit abject poverty or undue
hardship to persist in sections of its population."[36]

Chief Adebo, the former Nigerian permanent representative to the United Nations and head of the Interim
Wage Award Commission preceding the Udoji Commission,
urged the FMG to use the resources of the country to
the benefit of the masses. In a remark at an exhibi-
tion in Abeokuta he contended that revenue from national resources should be used to develop the country
because such development would foster everlasting
unity among various ethnic groups. He was critical of
the present situation in the country, which "afforded

only some few people to swim in abundant wealth while
the population swells in abject poverty."[37]

According to press reports, the students of Ahmadu
Bello University began an indefinite boycott of classes
over what they regarded as inadequate response to the
problems of the masses. They passed a resolution that
reads:

> We reject the Udoji recommendation in its
> totality and call on the Federal Government
> to make known a categorical statement on the
> progress so far made by the Armed Forces Sal-
> ary Review Commission.
>
> The Federal Government should embark, as a
> matter of urgency, on a programme towards
> providing free and adequate medical facili-
> ties, pipe-borne water, electricity, adequate
> and efficient infra-structure to the rural,
> and as now, forgotten areas.
>
> The Federal Government should embark on mas-
> sive importation of agro-industrial machin-
> eries, fertilizers and sell the same to
> farmers at subsidised rates.
>
> The Federal Government should waive community
> and council taxes and give more subsidies to
> the various local authorities.
>
> In order to justify the benefits of the rev-
> enue realised from the oil boom, free edu-
> cation should be provided at all levels.
>
> We call for the abrogation of decree 24.[38]

In an open letter accompanying their resolution to
Gowon (copies of which were sent to the vice-
chancellor of the university, Professor Ishaya Audu,
the Interim Common Service Agency, and the Public
Service Review Unit of the Federal Ministry of Establishment) the union gave the federal government forty-
eight hours to reply to their resolution.

On January 18 the Cabinet Office issued a statement denying that salaries and wages of the members
of the armed forces had been substantially increased
as a result of Udoji awards. The office explained

that a committee set up to make proposals for realigning wages and salaries of the armed forces had not yet submitted its report to the government. Four days later, in an address of welcome to the newly appointed federal commissioners in Lagos, General Gowon also denied the rumor.[39]

Consider a passage written by the political editor of a Nigerian newspaper concerning a fictitious Wretched Peoples Union. It is quoted verbatim in the note because in a political system somewhat intolerant of open criticism, such fictitious discourse carried ominous implications for political stability to the extent that it tends to accurately represent veiled articulation of serious disaffection.[40]

Another measure of a government's seriousness vis-à-vis the goal of equity is housing for the majority. The government had been somewhat successful with rent control, but needed to move away from demand control to supply management. The crux of the problem was the paucity of adequate housing supply in the major cities and the high cost of building materials. If domestic production of building materials could be increased, together with the reduction and elimination of various duties on these commodities, the housing problem could be eased. The FMG in fact embarked upon this policy, and quite a number of houses were completed. The signal for construction of low-income housing for urban workers was given in the 1972 Independence Day speech by General Gowon. Identifying the acute shortage of housing as one of the major social problems facing the nation, he said that his government would build 54,000 new houses in the federation— at a cost of Ł80 million. Of these, 10,000 would be built in Lagos while 4,000 would be built in each of the other states. The general noted that the huge amount allocated for the low-cost housing was insignificant compared with the hardship and suffering to which the working population in urban areas was subjected. But he promised, "This is not a once-for-all exercise as the Federal Government is firmly committed to providing these low-cost houses for working population of urban areas." As evidence of his determination to improve the lot of workers, the head of state pointed to the plan to set up workers and civil service cooperatives in the very near future.[41]

C. O. Lawson, chairman of the Federal Housing

Authority and head of the Nigerian Civil Service,
announced a more ambitious plan in early 1975. Accord-
to Mr. Lawson, by 1980 there would be two million housing
ing units built by the new federal housing scheme. By
the end of 1975 there would be 40,000 units. He des-
cribed the housing plan as a "welfare programme which
will usher in peaceful social revolution at a minimum
cost."[42]

    Generally, the military government's difficulties
derive in part from apparently contradictory policies.
In the attempt to please everyone, a government policy on a simple matter such as housing, when applied
to all without careful thought, will not have the
desired effect. In 1973, a year after announcing the
low-cost housing project, the FMG indicated that it
would assume full responsibility for housing senior
officials. This, the government explained, involved
direct negotiation with landlords and the willingness
to pay from three to five years' advance rent to
reserve houses for senior government officials. The
proposed rent entitlements were: for Scale A officers,
₦100 a month, with the officer paying ₦13 a month; for
Scale A(u), ₦140 a month, with the officer paying ₦25.
This proposal raised an outcry from the public and
from junior civil servants,[43] who calculated that this
amounted to a 56.49 percent pay raise for officers on
Scale A and a 22.6 percent raise for those on Scale
A(u).[44] As a result of these protests the government
replaced the plan with a modified one that would not
put the government in the position of directly nego-
tiating with landlords. Nor would it allow advance
payment of rent. It did provide for rent subsidies
to the following categories of workers:

Group 5 and below	₦60 a month
Group 6 to 8	₦50 a month
A Scale	₦40 a month

Female officers would be eligible for rent subsidies
provided they were not married to federal officers
entitled to rent subsidies.[45]

    Had the plan to pay advance rent to landlords
become policy, it would have put middle-level and

low-income workers at a disadvantage in the competi-
tion for limited housing. Although the revised policy
still puts this class of workers at some disadvantage,
since it provided for intensifying government housing
construction for senior service quarters and actively
encouraging officers to build their own houses (by
awarding housing loans), it would increase the supply
of houses and also free some houses for middle-level
workers.

One of the primary economic policies of the FMG
was apparently the attainment of economic nationalism.
One of the instruments set up to attain this goal was
the Nigerian Enterprise Decree, an attempt to encourage Nigerians to participate more actively in the modern sector. It reserved some business exclusively for
Nigerians (schedule 1) and stipulated that Nigerians
should have at least 40 percent of the share in the
others (schedule 2). The Enterprises Promotion Board
(NEPB) and the Capital Issues Commission (CIC) were
created to implement the policy. Businesses under
schedule 1 were offered for sale to Nigerians under
the auspices of the NEPB, and those under schedule 2
were floated under the prices fixed by the CIC. The
Bank of Commerce and Industry was set up to give
assistance to competent Nigerians who wanted to participate in businesses under schedule 2.

This policy could presumably function as an
instrument not only of economic growth but also of
economic development—one which would allow Nigerians
to share in their economic growth. If operated at its
best it would make it possible for the working class
and others to be absorbed into the ownership class.
Unfortunately, without thorough and extremely judicious planning it might not be a meaningful redistrib-
utive tool. Rather, it might replace foreign monop-
olists, thus creating a new class of "domestic
imperialists."

One authority has contended that it is indeed the
case that the Nigerian Enterprise Decree by default,
made it possible to substitute expatriate imperialism
with domestic imperialism. He asserts that "although
indigenisation may have succeeded in redistributing
wealth between expatriates and Nigerians, it surely
has created more inequalities in the distribution of
wealth among Nigerians. Very few companies offered
their shares to the general public through the Stock

Exchange, and nearly all the businesses under schedule one and the majority of those under schedule two of the decree were sold through private treaties and mostly to the friends and acquaintances of the companies or their brokers." Further, "there is no evidence that the reduction or abolition of import and excise duties has resulted in lower prices which would pass the benefits on to the consumers."[46] Although one can point to the correlation between these policies and the reduction in the inflation rate from the 9.5 percent of 1971/72 to the 3.0 percent of 1972/73—a rather dramatic drop—this may in fact be a spurious correlation in view of such reports as the following.

> The official price of Portland Cement has risen by 10 per cent. A bag of cement now sells at 2.20 naira instead of 2 naira in Lagos, Ikorodu, Abeokuta, Ilaro, and Ifo. The prices in other areas will rise accordingly. Last April, the Federal Government abolished the excise duty on cement and reduced duty on imported cement by 10 per cent. The import duty on gypsum was also reduced. West African Portland Cement says that the effect of these measures were wiped out by increases in freight rates, cost of spare parts and steel production arising from higher oil prices.[47]

The National Supply Company was criticized for concentrating on an area where it had no initiative. "All it can do is to place orders and then wait for supplies."[48] It is therefore not immune from worldwide inflation.

Although the Price Control Board was sometimes successful in combatting inflation, it was prevented from doing more in this area because while it could fix prices it could not enforce them. Essential commodities tended to be scarce, and those selling them found themselves in a monopolistic posture in which they could dictate the prices. The board did not have available to it the requisite machinery to police the chain of middlemen.

Under the circumstances a policy of demand management and price control will not be efficacious unless it is somehow coupled with a policy of supply management. The National Supply Company would have to concentrate upon supplying commodities over which it could exercise control and initiative, that is, in the area of local production and distribution. "The company should adopt a marketing board approach to stimulate the growth, collection and distribution of locally produced goods in the same way as the marketing boards were used during the colonial era to a great advantage to stimulate the production and marketing of export produce goods." Similarly, "rather than confine incentive and farmer prices to export producing farmers it should offer incentives also to the production and distribution of those (farmers) engaged in local food stuffs."[49]

On the whole there is evidence to support the military government's claim of concern not only for economic growth but also for economic development. Unhappily, there is also ample evidence that government policies directed toward the latter did not always have the desired effect. There are various reasons for this. Some of these have little to do with the government's capacities or capabilities—consider the spending behavior of the workers following the Udoji awards. Others are directly related to the lack of adequate executive capabilities and of judicious and thorough planning. An example of the latter would be the unanticipated consequences of the so-called Indigenisation Decree relative to its impact on economic distribution. One must add to these the dangers of overbureaucratization, the lack of coordination, and the tendency of a few competent top civil servants to overspread themselves and overtax their own capabilities. Finally, the increasing lack of proper trust between the governors and the governed continued to be a handicap.

CHAPTER THREE

Perception of Development Performance of the Regime:
Students, Lecturers, Farmers, and Traders

In sub-Saharan Africa the universities, with the exception of Fourah Bay College, were created after World
War II. In some ways then they, like the armed forces,
could be regarded as essentially colonial institutions. Edward Shils was right when he called the university students ex-officio members of the intellec-
tual class. Certainly in the days when the pen was
decidedly mightier than the sword the students' self-
image, as well as others' image of them, was that they
belonged to the ruling elite. Student political agi-
tation during the colonial days was an extremely rare
phenomenon. But times, and conditions, changed.

The primary concern here is with students' perception of the performance of the military regime.
Direct indicators such as student strikes and actions
are important, and questionnaires are helpful. The
general relationship between the military regime and
the students, as borne out by the perceptions and ver-
bal pronouncements of each, are equally relevant. A
necessary first step is to examine the development of
the role and the image of students vis-à-vis government authorities and government actions, for these
have undergone critical metamorphic developments.

Mabel Shegun, the first Nigerian woman graduate
of Nigeria's premier university, the University of
Ibadan, recalls an incident in 1949. Following the
shooting of Enugu miners who had gone on strike for
better working conditions, a fellow student tried to
propel an extremely lethargic student body to political action.

A tall bespectacled student rose to speak.
He said, "This is a most wicked act. The
British are ill-treating us because we are

under them.   They would not do this to their
own miners.   They do it to our people because
they feel nobody will ask them.   But we must
ask them.   We must not keep quiet.   The blood
of the miners will be on our heads if we
don't do something.   We must do something
even if it costs us our lives."   His voice
had risen as he became worked up and his audi-
ence was getting carried away.   There were
shouts of "good talk, good talk."   But when
he said, "Who is ready to die for his country?"
his question was greeted with silence.   "Well,
we must do something," the student ended
lamely and sat down.   In the end a two minute
silence was decided upon at lecture time and
a fast the next day.   But the student who had
suggested it was seen smuggling bread and
corned beef into his room.[1]

No, there was no boycott of lectures and no fast,
although there might have been two minutes of silence.
One could argue without fear of serious contradiction
that this account is characteristic of the posture and
attitude of university students on matters of deep
societal concern, not only during the colonial period,
but until the beginning of the Nigerian civil war.[2]

There was one notable exception, however—the
student demonstration against the Anglo-Nigerian
Defense Pact, which the university students felt com-
promised Nigerian independence and the foreign policy
principle of "neutrality."[3]   Otherwise the students
directed their attention only toward matters that they
construed as having an immediate impact on their own
welfare.   Even here demonstrations were infrequent,
because in earlier days Nigerian institutions of
higher learning had been very few indeed and the number of students in them only a few hundred.   They were
pampered and privileged, and there was little reason
to protest.   Generally the students were happy to
await the time when they would be absorbed into the
societal establishment.   There was still room for
them at the top.   Perhaps it should be added that they
shared in the primordial malaise that pervaded the
other sectors of society.   There was a real absence of
internal cohesion, and if one accepts Lewis Coser's
functional analysis of conflict it is not surprising
that the first successful effort at political involvement came in the area of foreign affairs.[4]

Until the middle of the Nigerian civil war,
Nigerian university students continued to look at education from the personalistic and instrumental point
of view. The impression they gave was that the university diploma was a necessity, not for patriotic
service, but as an instrument of social mobility.
They were overwhelmingly eager and anxious to get cars
and to join the senior service without seriously questioning societal values.[5]

What has the military regime expected from the
universities? General Gowon, at a "foundation" ceremony at the University of Ibadan, discussed the role
of the universities and university students. He
asserted that in the past there had been a lack of
student interest or involvement in societal affairs;
the university was only concerned with knowledge. He
went on:

> The modern society expects a great deal more
> from a university and rightly so. A univer-
> sity is now regarded as a public institution
> on which a substantial proportion of the
> nation's financial resources are to be
> expended. . . . The people are no longer
> interested in any institution which isolates
> itself from society or is unable to contrib-
> ute more directly to the growth and develop-
> ment of that society. One of the challenges
> of the future is the extent to which our uni-
> versities can meet the needs and aspirations
> of the society which they were established
> to serve. . . .

But Gowon praised the students for not becoming "too"
involved:

> I would like to congratulate the students of
> our universities for the comparatively high
> sense of responsibility which they have shown
> in the midst of the formidable exhibition of
> student discontent and unrest in the univer-
> sity world. . . . It will be an abuse of priv-
> ilege to visit upon the university grievances
> which may well be against the shortcomings of
> society as a whole, or to pitch a destructive
> battle in a university which is run with the
> monies from taxpayers and with assistance
> from abroad. Our students have been sensible

enough not to be misguided by many of
their counterparts elsewhere.[6]

Although student unrest was not commonplace in Nigeria
at this time, the Federal Military Governmant had
already begun to treat students gingerly, holding the
view that student disaffection could ignite the rest
of the country. In its pronouncements the government
stressed the importance of order, as opposed to change.
"The future of our great country depends on you the
youth to cultivate a sense of belonging, of understanding and tolerance." "The nation expects you and
it behooves you to be responsible." "The nation looks
to you for its future stability and you must not fail
us."[7]

The students were unwittingly politicized during
the civil war, but this politicization was an accept-
able one since it was generally supportive of the government's war effort and uncompromising in its vilifi-
cation of outside powers perceived as imperialist.
For example, during the war student demonstrators protested foreign governments' policies regarding Biafra.[8]

But the war also caused the students considerable
financial hardship. They could now empathize with
those less fortunate than they. In addition, the termination of the war and the announcement of the continuation of military rule until 1976 meant a more or
less permanent change in societal power and authority
structures. Less-educated men, without university
degrees but with military uniforms, would continue to
cement their control of political power and their role
as political masters. The students were very critical
and suspicious of this.[9]

Following the successful termination of the war
the president of the National Union of Nigerian Students (NUNS), speaking on behalf of university students, asked that the state of emergency be lifted.
He argued that with the end of the war it had outlived
its usefulness. If military rule was to end in 1976
it was necessary to begin political discussions and
education regarding the future of Nigeria and Nigerians.
The students arrogated to themselves and the press a
critical role in these discussions. They called on
all to forge a new identity in "our struggle for academic freedom, social justice and the building of a
truly great Nigeria."[10]

The students thus gave a clear signal that with
the end of the civil war they were not going to revert
to the apolitical posture of the colonial era. Nor
would they limit their political concerns to foreign
affairs as they had done throughout the civil-war
period. They now saw themselves as the patrons and
architects of a new Nigeria. Increasingly, however,
the military government saw them as potential or real
adversaries. The crux of the matter is that most university students (as I will show) have very little
respect for the military, considering them to be
largely ignorant, corrupt, dishonest, and incompetent.

Elsewhere I have discussed in detail the relationship between these two groups.[11] These relationships
are of concern here only insofar as they reflect students' confidence or lack of confidence in government
performance. Before discussing three critical cases
that address themselves squarely to this issue, some
important factors should be noted: the increasing disappearance of primordial factors that contributed to
the nature and extremely limited parameter of student
political concern up to the end of the civil war; the
increment and mutuality of militancy, which had become
the instrument of interest articulation for both the
military regime and the university students; and the
fact that as the university students broaden their
political concern so do others demonstrate their empa-
thy for them and their position.[12] A few army officers
have referred to the students as "the only political
party in Nigeria today."[13] Some students have said
that Nigeria has a single-party system--"the military."
These are obviously exaggerations, but the implication
of the statements remains. This is the metamorphic
development in the overall relations between the two
groups.

Now let us address ourselves to more specific
postures and actions that reflect, directly or indirectly, the students' perception of military performance relative to the goals and policies to which the
military regime committed itself. The government policies with salient heuristic implications for our concern are

the creation of the Nigerian Youth Service Corps,

The decision of the FMG to continue in power
after 1976, and

the Udoji Commission report and the government
acceptance of it.

The government decided to create a National Youth
Service Corps (NYSC), scheduled to begin in June 1973.
Its purposes were "to bring our young men and women
together with the primary objective of inculcating in
them a sense of discipline, dedication, national pride
and consciousness, through employment in nationally
directed and productive activities." General Gowon
saw it as a potent instrument for national unity, cut-
ting across political, social, state, religious, and
ethnic loyalties. "It was designed," he said, "to
afford Nigerian youth the chance for rendering selfless and honest service to the nation."[14]

As originally proposed the program called for a
two-year term of compulsory service for college graduates up to the age of thirty. Members of the corps
would be provided with free accommodation and with
stipends of ₦100 per month. Graduates would not be
allowed to take on permanent employment until the completion of their service. Members of the NYSC would
build roads, bridges, schools, and clinics. They
would work on farms and help in other ways to push
rural development. They were to reside in rural,
300-acre camps across the country in groups of 500.
Each camp would be expected to be partially self-
sufficient in food and, under professional guidance,
would build its own living quarters.[15]

There were student demonstrations against the
project in four of the six Nigerian universities. The
students, most of whom were from the southern states,
understood the implication of the NYSC conscription in
terms of its effect on their own preference for employment in urban areas and southern states.

The students' objections rested on a number of
points. First, they were unhappy about the absence
of details on the project; the government did not elab-
orate beyond the bare outline provided in several
addresses by General Gowon.[16] Second, the students
maintained that the government had not given them the
opportunity for meaningful input.

Both the Federal Public Service Commission and
the universities were required to offer advice on the
scheme. In accordance with this instruction an

interuniversity workshop was held under the sponsor-
ship of the vice-chancellors of the universities.
This Ibadan workshop, held on February 23, 1973, was
attended by NUNS representatives. A crisis was sig-
naled when a student representative walked out of the
meeting because, according to him, "the FMG and Committee of Vice-Chancellors have taken vital decisions
affecting students without bringing students into
decision-making."[17] The students also asserted that
they had been kept in the dark with regard to the
terms of service and that the FMB was required to dis-
cuss matters with them.

Although it is true that as of 1973 the Nigerian
government subsidized university education to the tune
of 80 to 90 percent,[18] only about 50 percent of the
university students received state and federal schol-
arships. According to NUNS, the other 50 percent
believed it is unfair to impose compulsory NYSC on
all. This constituted another student objection. The
students therefore demanded that free university education be a prerequisite of the new program. They
demanded the initiation of free university education
in September 1973 and the conscription of the first
graduates into NYSC in June 1974. As an alternative,
the government could make university education at all
levels free immediately.

A fourth objection revolved around a general lack
of trust in the sincerity and performance of the military leadership. The students had become increasingly
dissatisfied with the new ruling class. They carried
placards which read, "Top Men Enjoying Oil Boom, Young
Ones Suffer," "Service Corps or Suffering Corps?"
"Enlist Prominent Military Men Also," and "Gowon:
Beware of Advisors!"[19] These placards speak for the
students' lack of faith in the selflessness of the
current Nigerian military regime.

At first it seemed that the students would win
their fight for a postponement because the states'
public service commissions were recruiting graduates
for employment the next year despite the NYSC issue.
Many 1973 graduates had in fact secured employment.
Also, given the nature of extended families in Nigeria
and the role the members tend to play in the financing
of education for the nonscholarship students, one
would have thought that parents of these students
would not be passive about such a "semi-philanthropic"

organization as the NYSC.

The president of NUNS declared, "The promulgation of any decree on NYSC without prior discussion with us as promised and without the acceptance of our recommendations shall not be binding on us."[20]   The students demanded the introduction of free university education; direct consultation with the FMG; and a voluntary, not compulsory, NYSC. In the end the only concession granted by the FMG was a reduction of the length of service from two years to one year. The intransigence of the FMG in this matter indicates the significance it attached to the NYSC.

Student opposition to the NYSC was violent and unequivocal. At the University of Lagos students wrecked a number of cars, smashed windows, and stripped General Gowon's name from the university library name plate. At other universities students boycotted classes and demonstrated against government policy. Despite all this, some 2,600 students were drafted into the NYSC in June 1973.

My view is that the students were not opposed to the NYSC per se. During the war they had requested the military to draft students into the armed forces. The opinions some students expressed when interviewed indicated that they doubted the sincerity of the military regime. Some believed that the NYSC was a punitive policy designed to produce a less idealistic student body. It was generally agreed that there was no special reason that only university students should be requested to sacrifice. (Their placards clearly indicate this.)

A questionnaire conducted by NYSC headquarters after the first year of its operation suggests that a substantial percentage of its first graduates would be willing to take up employment in other states. Federal Public Service Commission data shows, however, that out of 300 NYSC graduates offered jobs outside of their states of origin, only 131 accepted.[21]   This does not indicate an overwhelming change. Indeed, the NYSC had given students the feeling that they were performing national service comparing favorably to that offered by any other Nigerian group, although they were the only ones mandated to perform national service. It is therefore difficult to avoid the conclusion that the students' intensified political

assertiveness was not linked to the new role they had
been forced to perform.

In his speech on the fourteenth anniversary of
Nigerian independence the head of state announced,
contrary to expectations and his October 1, 1971 promise, that the military would continue in power. He
said that the 1976 target date given four years earlier
for the return to a normal constitutional government
had been premature. He and the military hierarchy had
thought that after a bloody civil war and much human
sacrifice Nigerians would have learned a lesson. Unfortunately, those aspiring to political leadership in
postmilitary rule had learned little from these
experiences.[22]

It is noteworthy that the general continued to
promise that proven cases of corruption would be
firmly dealt with; that armed forces salaries would be
reviewed; that the constitution of the country would
be reviewed; and that census results would be published as soon as ready. It will become evident that,
although there were no immediate student demonstrations regarding these unexpected changes, the demonstrations that erupted in 1975 were clearly addressed
to these very issues and indicated the reactions of
the students. It should also be noted that the "events"
referred to in the General's speech, rationalizing the
military government's decision not to abrogate power
and authority as it had promised, centered around two
issues that the Gowan regime had used to justify military
rule following the end of the Nigerian civil war.
Specifically, the military had promised to have the
census figures ready and to "eradicate corruption."
In a way, the general had opened up the debate in his
convocation speech at Ahmadu Bello University in
December 1972. At that time he invited open discussion with regard to the political future of the country.

The students seemed bewildered, therefore, that
their role in forcing the resignation of J. S. Tarka,
the federal commissioner of communication who was
accused of corruption and nepotism by Daboah, was
apparently unappreciated by the FMG.[23] The reluctance
of police authorities to vigorously pursue its investigation of this matter left Nigerians with an unfa-
vorable impression of the military regime with regard

to its seriousness about self-appointed policy tasks.

    In a similar incident Aper Aku accused Governor
Gomwalk of Benue-Plateau of nepotism and corruption.
After failing in his attempts to cause an investigation through the normal channels of authority, Aku,
like Daboah, swore an affidavit. Unlike Daboah, however, Aku was put in detention without trial and without a police investigation of the case. As of 1975
neither Tarka nor the governor had been brought to
court to answer charges sworn to in affidavits against
them. In the case of Governor Gomwalk, General Gowon
exonerated him from allegations of wrongdoing. "I am
now satisfied after listening to explanations and having had time to check all the references provided by
Mr. Gomwalk that he has not been guilty of any wrong
doings as alleged by Mr. Aku in his affidavit." Gowon
warned the courts and the press not to allow themselves to be used as instruments of blackmail against
highly placed public officials with the view to tar-
nishing their image. He said that the FMG would resist
any attempt by any person in the country to discredit
the military.[24]

    Under public pressure the head of state invited
Gomwalk to Lagos to answer the allegations. Between
the time of the invitation and Gomwalk's exoneration
by the head of state, the police and the army stormed
and searched the campus of the University of Ibadan.
The university administrators, professors, and students were bewildered. When Gowon was questioned
about this action he said that he was fully aware of
the operation, claiming that "this is part of national
security." What is interesting is that nothing was
found and nobody detained. General Gowon stated that
the anticorruption campaign was ill-motivated, aimed
at discrediting him, his close lieutenants, and his
government. We thus have the interesting situation
in which the students were suspected for helping the
regime to accomplish one of its declared major programs and policies.[25] The motives of the press were
impugned, the judiciary warned, and the students
harassed.

    An editorial commented that a threat of the
inspector general of police against the Nigerian press
is typical—it happens whenever the press crusades
against government wrongdoing. Although the press had
become accustomed to threats by government officials,

the editorial wondered whether the judiciary was also "used to such warnings."[26] What the Nigerian students saw was the inspector general of the police (the highest police officer, member of the Supreme Military Council and Federal Executive Council) warning the press for "doing its duty."[27] The head of state who had called for vigilance against corruption had "warned" the judiciary and the supposedly "ill-motivated" Nigerians[28] who, judging from letters to the editor, were a very substantial number and representative of all walks of life.

The relatively conservative students of the Ahmadu Bello University joined their counterparts in the southern states in their appeal for the release of Aku.[29] The Nigerian universities and other institutions of higher learning embarked upon lecture boycotts, memorandums to the FMG, and other methods to force the government to release Aku and Tai Solarin who, like others, had been detained either for doing what the FMG professed to desire or for questioning the government for not abiding by its promise to relinquish power.

The point here is not that corruption is ipso facto antidevelopment.[30] Rather, if anticorruption is declared by the government as one of its major policies, then it is not unfair for that item to enter into the analysis of government performance, whether from an objective or a subjective vantage point. In the case of both Aku and Solarin, the FMG had to give in to the persistent demands of the students. The students generally remained united in their causes and were supported by the newspapers in their demands. Their methods did not always meet with overwhelming approval, however.[31] But as the *Daily Times* pointed out, the government was largely to blame. There is a communication gap between the government and the people, the paper commented. In part this is because in the absence of a parliament government business is conducted at Federal Executive Council, Supreme Military Council, and permanent secretaries' committee meetings. The people know of government thinking and activities from airport press conferences and official statements, one-way communication that does not provide the citizens with requisite channels through which their thinking and reactions can pass to the government.

Nigerians delight in having a say in how they

are governed. Happily, the Head of State
said in his last October message to the
nation that advisory committees would be
set up. The *Daily Times* adds that deliberative assemblies should be set up at the
federal and state levels. In the circumstances of today the members have to be
nominated from all shades of opinion and
all walks of life. In the period between
now and the time of return to democratic
rule, the deliberative assemblies will provide the forum for representatives of the
federal and state governments and the nominated representatives of the people to
exchange views of public affairs.[32]

   Now let us turn to the students' perception of
the Udoji recommendations and the government's white
paper. Following the publication of the new wage salaries the students in the Technical Institute, beginning with the Polytechnic at Kaduna, protested what
they considered the low priority given to technical
education. The students at the Ahmadu Bello University began an indefinite boycott of lectures (discussed in chapter 2). They called for the publication of military salaries and the redistribution of
resources so that the condition of the rural masses
could be improved. There were other demands among
what they called their concern for national issues.
Students at the universities of Ife, Ibadan, and
Lagos joined in "fighting in the interest of the suffering masses of this nation to justify their investment in our education."[33] The placards carried by
students in the demonstration showed the following
demands:

   1. that all corrupt officials of governments
      be probed;

   2. that money in New York and Switzerland be
      brought back home;

   3. that Emergency Decree 34 be abrogated;

   4. that the press not be gagged;

   5. that the 1973 census figures be released;

6. that the Udoji recommendations not be
   implemented;

7. that the inadequacies of the Price Control
   Board and the Nigerian National Supply
   Company be rectified;

8. that an equitable revenue allocation formula be introduced;

9. that a constituent assembly of peasants,
   workers, students, and professionals be
   set up;

10. that there be a resettlement program for
    beggars and free education and free medi-
    cal service for all;

11. that a comprehensive economic plan for
    full employment be introduced;

12. that a democratic organization be set
    up to guarantee a free press, an indepen-
    dent judiciary, and independent autono-
    mous universities. [34]

Following several days of lecture boycotts, the academic senates of the universities of Ibadan, Lagos,
and Ife decided to close the universities until further notice. On February 22, 1975,the Committee of
Vice-Chancellors of Nigerian Universities announced
conditions for the readmission of students to
institutions closed down as a result of student unrest.
The affected students would have to be prepared to
make full restitution from their individual pockets
for any damage done to property in the institutions,
to reaffirm their matriculation oath and promise that
in the future they would not employ violence in seek-
ing redress, and to try not to disrupt normal academic
activities. Furthermore, the committee condemned any
undisciplined and violent acts on university campuses.
But five days later the FMG, acting in what appears to
to be an extraconstitutional capacity, countermanded
the university authority with the order that the three
universities not reopen. It believed that the vice-
chancellors' order was premature. [35] Public statements
by several military governors and by the head of state
clearly indicate the regime's belief that these protests were externally motivated.

NUNS expressed grave concern over the FMG's coun-
termand of the university senates' decision. "All
that students have tried to do is to tell the government in simple terms that our [the FMG's] priorities
are misplaced. . . . What the government should do now
is to try and settle the issues raised and take the
students into confidence rather than trying to find
external influences where there are none." The students insisted in their message that a new way of com-
municating their opinions to the government had to be
found. They claimed to be responsible and mature
citizens interested in the "radical progress of this
country." Their message went on to say:

> Although events have moved so fast to the
> extent that well placed Nigerians continue
> to see students as tools and stooges who
> can't reason on their own, the NUNS wants
> to assure the government and the Nigerian
> public that a majority of Nigerian students
> are very mature men and women. . . . What
> is necessary now is an era of meaningful
> dialogue between the government and the
> students, or else one would continue to
> misunderstand the other at the nation's
> expense. [36]

Meanwhile the students at the University of Lagos said
that they would not return to the university unless
their detained leaders, Tayo Sowunmi and Biodun Oduwole,
were released. The students warned that detention of
student leaders was the "latest wrong move" by the
government.

The *Daily Times* considered the FMG order ill
advised. [37] Four influential university professors
protested the government action. [38] The Nigerian Association of University Teachers (NAUT) joined in the
appeal. It regretted the indefinite closure of the
universities and the "circumstances and manner of such
a decision by the Federal Government." The teachers
said that although they were aware that the situation
in the country was peculiar in view of the military
rule, Nigerian universities must uphold and preserve
academic freedom. The association made a nine-point
recommendation to the FMG:

> 1) to appreciate the gravity of the situation
>   in the closure of the universities and the

serious effects it has on other sister universities;

2) to recognize and respect the senate in its capacity as the highest academic authority in the university;

3) to refrain from hindering the senates from exercising their authority in reopening at once the universities;

4) to limit intervention and its extent to such university matters as belong to the government or to which the competent university authorities invite government intervention;

5) to uphold, endorse and re-affirm academic freedom, and allow tolerance of ideas in an atmosphere of trust and confidence, and without being subjected to any interference, molestation, or penalization, even if these ideas are unacceptable to some constituted authority within or beyond the institution;

6) to recognize students as participants and contributors according to their proper roles in the affairs of the nation;

7) to welcome and arrange a dialogue with the NAUT on the issue at hand in order to achieve a rapproachment and thereby avoid unforeseen deterioration;

8) to reciprocate the gesture of the NAUT by releasing at once all persons detained in connection with the recent unfortunate incident and abjure all molestation in the resolution of this impasse;

9) to consider seriously that the appointment of a vice-chancellor of a university should be made by a process of democratic involvement of all members of the university community if the vice-chancellor is to command the respect and support of all.[39]

While joining those who were appealing to the FMG

to reopen the universities, the national officers of
NUNS pointed out that they disagreed with government
claims of its achievements while in office. "Whereas
rehabilitation programme is said to have been completed
in wartorn areas of the country, the situation of
schools and roads in war-affected areas is as disappointing as it is intolerable. To this end, we appeal
to the Federal Government to assist particularly war-
affected areas in rehabilitating their roads and
schools." The students expressed concern that five
years after the end of hostilities the fundamental
rights of property ownership were still being denied
some Nigerians. They called on the FMG to intervene
on the question of abandoned property with a view to
bringing an amicable settlement and final solution to
the issue.[40]

The judiciary avoided the appearance of partisan-
ship by appealing to the government to release all who
had been detained.[41] The press, along with its demand
for the lifting of the "state of emergency," called
for the release of those detained or requested that
they be brought to trial. As a result of all this
pressure the federal commissioner of information issued
an explanation regarding those who had been detained
by the government and the reasons for their detention.
He alleged that outside agitators, with motives inimical to the government, had been involved in the demonstrations. He further suggested that various groups
had been in "collusion" with the agitators. Impli-
cated in the supposed collusion were the medical students, who earlier had demonstrated against the Udoji
recommendations. In a statement to the press they
categorically denied the charges made against them by
the commissioner.[42] The Lagos students and vice-
chancellor also challenged the government statement.[43]

The five principal objectives of the FMG's four-
year-development plan were as follows:

1. A free and democratic society

2. A land of full and equal opportunity for
   its citizens

3. A just and equalitarian society

4. A united, strong, and self-reliant nation

5. A great and dynamic economy

As gleaned from their utterances and actions, the students believed that the government had not succeeded relative to points 1, 2, and 3. Their assessment vis-à-vis points 4 and 5 was varied. Questionnaire response indicated a feeling of respectable government performance on the last point, but subsequent actions and utterances of the students clearly indicate dissatisfaction even in this area.

The questionnaire responses will be taken up shortly, but first it should be noted that the changes in perception are a function of time. The questionnaires were taken before the clashes of government promises and action had become manifest. The government's nine-point plan of 1970 called for the following by 1976: nationally oriented political parties, eradication of corruption, a constituent assembly to examine the constitution, reorganization of the armed forces, a Revenue Reallocation Committee, an objective census, and implementation of a four-year national development plan.

It was obvious to the students that the indefinite postponement of a return to civilian rule and the continuing proscription of political organization made nationally oriented political parties impossible. Nor had the government eradicated corruption. In fact, both the students' motives and the anticorruption campaign of the press came under fire. A constitution was still promised at some future date, although the notion of a constituent assembly had been muted. The census undertaken by the FMG brought so much controversy that the exercise itself had been used by the government as an indication that it needed to continue in power. One could argue that this was direct admission of failure or a somewhat disappointing performance by the military hierarchy that established the deadline in the first place. The government accepted some of its failure relative to the execution of the development plan. The very fact that it had to extend the life of the plan to five years speaks for itself. The demonstrations and placards of the students show that they remained unconvinced that equity or development had occurred, although they believed that economic growth had taken place. The Nigerian students demanded

"full nationalisation of enterprises NOW and no indigenisation for the enrichment of a few."[44] It is possible although highly improbable that the nationaliza-
tion demand was based on the assumption that public
enterprise would offer more bureaucratic jobs than
private enterprise. This is highly improbable because
governmental jobs were no longer the top priority of
university graduates. Moreover, graduate unemployment
was not a problem given the NSYC. Finally, the other
demands are clearly of no direct self-interest to the
students. They wanted the government to "embark as a
matter of urgency on a programme towards providing
free, adequate and efficient infrastructure to the
rural and as now forgotten areas." They also called
for the "setting up of a Peoples Assembly made up of
democratically elected leaders of peasants, workers,
students, and professional associations to rule the
country."[45] They wanted comprehensive economic planning
to guarantee full employment and the utilization of
oil resources for free education at all levels.

At the time of the questionnaire (1971-72) the
specific policies disapproved of most vigorously
(high-low) were the government's financial educational
policies (82 percent), high military budget (70 percent), ineffective wage and price controls (48 percent), government's response to labor unrest and its
general handling of labor matters (42 percent).[46]
There is no doubt, given the nature of the objections
at that time, that if it were possible to enlarge the
list and ask the questions several years later, the
questionnaire would include the very items for which
the students had struck and demonstrated.

To return to the specific questions raised in
chapter 1, the answers to the questionnaire showed
that the students agreed that considerable economic
growth had occurred in Nigeria under the military
regime. Judging from the student actions and pronouncements discussed in this chapter, it is clear
that they did not think that development (equity) had
occurred. Their demands indicate this. At the time
of the questionnaire students were optimistic that
equity would emerge before 1976. Later they were
clearly pessimistic about this possibility. This is
poignantly illustrated by the fact that despite the
1975-80 ₦30,000 million plan, with provisions for
about a 250 percent increase in the number of university students, for an intake of 1,000 medical students

per year, and for a hospital-bed population ratio of
1:1,000, among other things, the university students
continued to make demands. The fact is that unlike in
1971, when student optimism was based on government
promises, the government's credibility had waned due
to the students' perception that it had failed to ful-
fill its promise of performance.

If education and social amenities provisions are
used as an index of social development, the questionnaire shows that 82 percent of the students believed
that government investment in education was a low priority. Of those interviewed, 70 percent resented the
high investment in the military budget. The majority
felt that the government's wage and price control
mechanisms were ineffective and that the burdens of
the poor therefore remained unalleviated. Only 14 percent
of the students interviewed had faith in the Nigerian
bureaucrat's capacity for high development.

The students believed overwhelmingly that neither
they nor the masses (farmers and workers) had been
given an opportunity for meaningful participation in
decision making, and 60 percent expressed very strong
opinions about the need to broaden participation so
that "the masses" could participate fully in Nigerian
political life. (Part of the objection against the
NYSC was the students' resentment that they had not
been given an opportunity for meaningful input on matters in which they alone were expected to make a
sacrifice.)

The strikes and violent demonstrations, which became the instrument of interest articulation by the
student, clearly reflect the absence of an effective
communication system and a feeling of alienation and
desperation. The military posture relative to the
university suggests a feeling of mutual alienation.
The students seemed insistent not only on ascertaining
that their limited interests are sufficiently represented but also on ensuring that the fruits of economic
growth are spread to all.

The barometer of student identity with various
governments, 1960-1972, is indicated by an order rank-
ing—lowest to highest—by the students themselves:

1964-65, 1972

1970-71 (following the end of the civil war)

1960, 1968-70

It is interesting that the students, using whatever
yardstick they elected, gave bad marks to both civilian and military regimes. It seems that the critical
judgment is whether the regime is credible and whether
or not it pursues policies with which one can identify.

The creation of the twelve-states structure and
the promise of the creation of more states drew the
highest praise from the students interviewed, with
76 percent believing that creating more states "would
be a political step in the right direction." Sixty
percent believed that between 1971 and 1972, unlike
later, the military government had succeeded in creating a dynamic economy and in bringing about economic
growth.

Lecturers' Assessment

The position and assessment of the lecturers generally parallel those of the students.[47] Here are
some interesting findings:

1. Whereas during the civil war 63 percent
   of the lecturers indicated close agreement
   with and general approval of the military
   regime's performance, only 9 percent of
   those interviewed in late 1972 gave favorable assessments.

2. Over 42 percent believed that there was a
   need for the military to show good example.
   They asserted that there was a wide gap
   between what the military regime professed
   and what it executed.

3. Almost all were very apprehensive because
   of a lack of communication between the
   citizens and the leadership of the military regime.

4. Approximately two-thirds of the lecturers
   believed that the military regime's attitude toward the academicians had changed
   for the worse following the successful
   termination of the civil war. Although
   several reasons were advanced for this

change in attitude, the most consistently mentioned was the lecturers' increasingly open and vocal criticisms of policies and performance.

The strike action by NAUT and the FMG reaction to it, together with actions suggestive of increasing governmental control of academe, further increased the chasm between lecturers and the military regime.[48] Here are a few random remarks of the lecturers relative to the military regime. "Less people feel pleasant about what the government is doing." "Lecturers are a bit jealous of the high benefits of soldiers." "The longer they [the military] stay, the more corrupt they become." "Shorten their reign and give government back to the civilians." "They [the military] should get out before their luck runs out."

Here are some other relevant findings:

1. The constitution of Nigeria should not be changed to allow the military to participate in politics, said 82 percent. They were, in other words, opposed to what later became known as a diarchy.

2. Strong opinions about broadening mass participation in Nigerian political life were expressed by 60 percent.

3. Only about 20 percent believed that by 1976 the Nigerian military government should have disposed of the most troublesome problems confronting the nation.

4. Only 14 percent had faith in the Nigerian bureaucrat's capacity for high performance.

What should have been most disturbing to the military regime is the fact that influential civilian political brokers and various religious groups also shared the students' assessment of government performance. That this was not disturbing could only be due to their belief, contrary to unambiguous evidence, that this was not the case. Consider the following evidence.

In the Adepoju death strike thousands of market women joined forces with the students. Following the

action of the government in countermanding the senates'
order to open up the universities, alumni of the University of Lagos not only attacked the FMG for uncon-
stitutionally grabbing power but viewed its action as
an attempt to silence independent thought and genuine
criticism. Significantly, they contended that "in a
society like ours where social justice is still a far-
fetched dream, university students would be negativis-
tic should they fail to agitate and appeal to the conscience of the nation.[49]

Examples abound showing that the students' perception of the military government's performance was
widely shared. First, a letter from the public opinion section of a newspaper:

> The explanation [*Daily Times*, March 4] by the
> new Federal Commissioner for Information,
> Mr. Edwin Clark, that the five detained per-
> sons--Mr. Anthony Engurube, Mr. C. O. Akinde,
> Dr. O. A. Akintunde, Dr. E. Madunagu, and
> Mr. Air Iyare--among other things, were the
> conniving force behind the present students'
> unrest in the country, makes interesting
> reading. To say that students were being
> used by some people is to assume that uni-
> versity students have no convictions of their
> own. If there is anything students should
> and do have in any country, it is intellect,
> which can be applied not only in reading
> their textbooks, but reasoning and reaching
> conclusions about the state of affairs of
> their society. African and particularly
> Nigerian leaders, whether elected or not,
> should do their best to accommodate opposing
> viewpoints or well-meaning criticism. It is
> in this way that meaningful progress and
> development can be achieved for the benefit
> of all citizens.[50]

Second, the Roman Catholic bishops of Nigeria at
their annual meeting called for "better life for people in rural areas through improved social services,
decentralisation of amenities and industries, rural
electrification and water schemes" as ways of cur-
tailing student and worker disaffection. The synod of
the Anglican bishops of the Province of West Africa
called upon the government "to see that the wealth
of the nation is distributed evenly and to the benefit

of all." According to newspaper accounts—not denied—
"The bishops associated themselves with all those who
have advocated for the provision of rural health, water
and electrification as well as for free education to
the secondary school level."[51]

Third, a notable and highly respected Nigerian,
Dr. Akanu Ibiam, said, "Cost of living is soaring
everyday and those who have not the food died and are
dying of hunger and starvation while medical services
throughout the land is anything but satisfactory particularly for the rural areas of our fatherland."[52]

It is this consonance of ideas that led the political editor of the *Daily Times* to remark:

> I come to the inevitable conclusion that
> while it is desirable for the government
> to search for those "hidden hands" that
> instigated the students, such preoccupa-
> tion should not blind it from the basic
> issues the students, and the bishops are
> raising. And these issues are what the
> students, the bishops and Mr. Akanu Ibiam
> are trying to highlight. And one only hopes
> that the government is listening.[53]

The conclusion is inevitable that if, despite strong
constraints on freedom of expression (Decrees 34 and
53), opinions seriously critical of government are
published, there must be an even higher degree of disaffection than one reads about. Most of what did
appear in all facets of the Nigerian press during this
period was quite critical of government policies and
development performance.

Farmers' Assessment

Even the farmers were becoming restless. They
were beginning to organize by refusing to sell their
products. The issue was not whether they could do this
indefinitely— the fact that they resorted to such
action is an indication of considerable alienation and
desperation. It constitutes a "vote of no confidence"
in the performance of government. The police in the
Western State warned farmers in certain areas against
setting up illegal roadblocks to prevent other farmers
from taking their products to market. The farmers

undoubtedly believed they were underpaid for their
crops, and they demanded increased social services
and reductions in the price of agricultural inputs.
In general they protested the high cost of living
in Nigeria.[54]

Newspaper reports of acute food shortages in
western Nigeria, a predominately agricultural area,
led one woman to remark, "We have never had it so
bad in peace time Nigeria." It is quite probable
that the acute shortage was partially due to the
farmers' campaign to stop foodstuffs from going to
the cities. Despite the fact that some farmers had
been convicted for their part in organizing or enforc-
ing this boycott, the food shortage continued, thus
attesting to the farmers' resolve to make their
point.[55]

In the Mid-West State, where the military government contended that in all sectors its performance had
been exemplary, the Mid-West Farmers Union made this
revealing statement: "The present situation where the
poor get poorer and the rich grab more is very unsatisfactory."[56]

The appraisal of the Western State Farmers Union
was not qualitatively different. In the Oyo area,
farmers formed a new organization, the Oyo and Dis-
trict Farmer Society. Its aim, according to its
spokesman, was to wage war against famine and not
against government. As they saw things, the farmers
have control only over their crops, and since they
have only limited yields it would be suicidal to sell
their crops and face starvation. Since they cannot
dictate the prices of building materials such as iron
sheets, cement, and planks, sold to them at exorbitant
prices, the only alternative was to withhold their
food. They called on government to cut the prices of
iron sheet from ₦36 to ₦11 and of cement from ₦72 to
₦22 per ton. Claiming that they did not want to
resort to violence, they asked the government to do
something about their plight.[57]

This represents a notable shift from a favorable
or optimistic to a less favorable perception. During
the first questionnaire Nigerian farmers were asked to
assess the performance of the military regime relative
to the government's declared objectives.[58] Below are
their responses.

Types of Performance	Positive Assessment (percent)	Negative Assessment (percent)	No Opinion (percent)
United Nigeria	52	8	40
Strong economy	62	12	26
Just society	62	18	20
Free society	28	65	3

Approximately three-fifths of the farmers interviewed at that time held the view that the military rulers in 1971 had embarked upon most of the tasks they promised. Of this number about 60 percent were optimistic that these tasks would be completed successfully and thus indicated faith in the capacity of government. The rest, however, were extremely skeptical.

Also on the positive side, the farmers indicated that late 1970 and early 1971 represented periods of highest satisfaction with the government; 1960 came second, and 1965 last of all. The farmers supported the government's wage and price control policy and would have liked to see it vigorously enforced (82 percent). About 76 percent supported the Agricultural Credit Corporation in principle. Approximately 88 percent supported commissions of inquiry into allegations of corruption because they saw this as a deterrent.

The general reservations that the farmers had about the Agricultural Credit Corporation and other lofty government policy ideals rested on their distrust of government officials. By 3 to 1, the farmers were opposed to increasing the military budget. In addition they were disappointed with the relative lack of consultation between the governors and the governed. In rank order they believed that farmers, women, workers, and students were extremely low participants in decision making (formal and informal).

With regard to Nigeria's immediate future the farmers opted for the following:

	Percent For	Percent Against
More power to the masses	70	22
A federal form of government	54	36
Non-involvement of military in government	70	22
Centralized government	36	60
Creation of more states	42	44

Interestingly, a majority of the farmers did not believe that the military would relinquish power in 1976 as promised. It is particularly revealing that as this was written the farmers who were withdrawing their products from the market came precisely from the area where the 1971 sample was drawn. It is obvious that government performance decreased considerably in the opinion of these farmers.

Traders' Perception

Let us now consider the traders. Tayo Adetola, the editor of a newspaper column, claimed that "to say that the cost of living in Nigeria has risen by at least 300 percent in the last five years would be no exaggeration." While she agreed that there had been efforts by the government to arrest the situation, "the sky-rocketing of prices continues to be a major national problem." She further contended that "before the release of the government's White Paper on Udoji, it was impossible for most Nigerians to have three square meals a day on their monthly income because of this steady rise in prices. This was particularly acute during the second half of November and also during December 1974."[59] Her contention is supported by news reports.[60] She held that things have not fared much better with the Udoji pay scales. "While most of the junior and some senior workers lavished their Udoji naira on 'wants' rather than 'needs' women have turned enemies of one another. Housewives versus market women, house maids versus their madams."[61]

     Consider these opinions of the market women who
are representative of several groups of market women
traders who sell food and other petty items. They are
quoted here at length because they represent the view
of their organizations, not only about inflation, but
also about what the government should do to solve the
problem.

     On inflation here is what Modupe Caxton-Martins,
president of the Lagos State Market Women's Association, had to say:

> The fault is not with us. We sell what we
> buy. Most of the foodstuff comes from the
> other states and it is these people that
> hold us to ransom. If the prices of goods
> go up from the source, we will be compelled
> to raise our own prices too. The people
> selling to us have devised all sorts of ways
> to make buying and selling difficult. The
> Iddo Market that used to be a place for
> wholesale activities now deals in retail
> trade. Most of the time the local market
> women cannot buy directly from the bulk sel-
> lers. They have to go through middlemen,
> and prices rise as goods pass from hand to
> hand. Government can only control prices
> if they ensure that we get goods at a reason-
> able price. Otherwise there is nothing they
> can do about the present situation.

What should government do to curb inflation? Mrs.
Caxton-Martins went on to suggest the following:

> The government farm settlements produce sub-
> stantial quantities of food items which are
> allegedly being sold to top officials of the
> various ministries and to their immediate
> relations, some of whom it is also alleged
> come to the markets to resell these items
> at inflated prices to the local market woman,
> who has to further inflate the prices because
> she must sell at a profit. If the situation
> whereby the products of the agricultural
> settlements circulate in very few hands is
> curbed and the authorities sell directly to
> the public, the present inflation will be

brought under control. The authorities can
do this by having stalls in the various mar-
kets where the members of the public can
buy directly from the agricultural people.

In addition she suggested that the handicapped be
trained in agriculture and encouraged "to make use
of crown lands to cultivate essential food items which
will be sold cheaply to the public." As a short-run
solution to the state of near-starvation Mrs. Caxton-
Martins advised: "The form of 'control' which existed
some 27 to 30 years ago in the days of Chief Falolu of
Lagos can still be practised. Then the government
sent agents into the interior, bought essential items
at reasonable prices and got the local market women to
resell them at prices where only minimal profit was
made."[62]

Alhaja Gatta, the representative of the Ebute Ero
Market Women, and other leaders of trading organizations, held similar views on these issues. Alhaja
Gatta emphasized that "apart from the rise in prices
from the source the mode of transportation has contributed in no small way to the present high prices."
She said that "when transportation of charcoal and
vegetables were done by boats they were paid something
like ₦1.75 per consignment. Now a lorry-load costs as
much as ₦60 from the source to Lagos." Commenting on
the allegation by housewives that market women have
associations where they dictate policies to members
and ensure that no one defaults, she said: "It is true
that we try to ensure uniformity in prices through our
association; but this is not done without taking into
consideration the buying prices. . . . There is no
hard and fast rule because there can be between five
kobo and 20 kobo difference in prices depending on
several other factors. For example, some people trade
with borrowed money and will want to sell their wares
in the quickest time possible in order to make whatever profit they can, and pay back their loans at a
reasonable time." She also mentioned that the problem
of population drift into the cities had greatly reduced
the farm hands and made labor difficult and expensive
to come by. "There is hardly cheap labour anywhere
now. Farmers now buy expensive machines to farm their
lands and this is all contributory to the high cost
from the source."[63]

The women's page editor of the *Daily Times* concluded:

"I think authorities should now come to the aid of the ordinary man in the street and save him from slow but sure death as a result of gradual starvation. Something must be done and urgently too."[64]

Both later and during the interview traders denied that the government had pursued a policy of equity. What the petty traders referred to as "common men" were seen as ignored. These traders should, of course, be distinguished from the big Nigerian entrepreneurs who were beneficiaries of the Nigerian Indegenisation Decree. Incidentally, both the Nigerian petty traders and the members of the Nigerian Chamber of Commerce have been critical of wage and price controls and the Nigerian Price Control Board. Chief Fajemirokun and the Chamber of Commerce continued to call either for the scrapping of the Price Control Board or the representation of business on the board.

There seems to be some consistency in the traders' perception of the government's economic performance. At the time of the interview 86 percent agreed that the government had not ended inflation, 66 percent disagreed with government wage and price controls, and 75 percent said that wage and price controls could not work because of government corruption and unrealistic price ceilings. About 86 percent believed that the policy of equalitarianism had not been pursued.[65] The conclusion indirectly expressed was that the prices of goods cannot be controlled effectively unless the government produces goods. In short, the traders were in favor of supply rather than demand management.

CHAPTER FOUR

Perception of Development Performance of the Regime:
Press and Labor

In examining the perception of the press relative to
the performance of the Gowon military regime it is
necessary to mention the considerable handicap under
which it operates. Two decrees that are almost
Draconian are germane—Decree 21 of 1968 and Decree 53
of 1969. The first severely curtailed the right to
strike, and the other totally abolished that right.
As these decrees relate to the press they stipulated
that it is "an offence to publish in newspaper, radio
and television or any other means of mass communication anything which can cause public alarm or industrial unrest." Clearly it is thereby an offence to
carry news of public strikes and lockouts. The decrees
also grant the right of arbitrary detention to the
inspector general of police, the chief of staff of the
army, and the chief of staff of supreme headquarters,
suspending habeas corpus, the traditional instrument
for challenging unlawful detention in such cases.
Almost to the last man the Nigerian journalists
abhorred these decrees, and there were endless and
incessant calls for their abrogation. Generally the
government was adamant on this score.

During the Nigerian civil regime the efficacy of
the press as well as its objectivity suffered tremen-
dously due to several factors, among them parochialism
and the primordial sentiments of the press and its
management. These are not really of concern here, but
the increasing disappearance of these liabilities in
the Nigerian press needs mentioning. Sometime in the
middle of the Nigerian civil war the press underwent
a metamorphosis, and a self-appointed new role and
function emerged. What was the self-image of the
Nigerian press with regard to its role and accomplishments?

> The press had to constantly remind the new
> masters of their pledges to the electorate.
> . . . The press [after independence, during
> the civil war] promptly reflected the opin-
> ions of the masses and castigated the prof-
> ligate ministers for despoiling the treasury.
> Politicians reacted swiftly. There were
> attempts to muzzle the press and to make
> ministerial appointments sacrosanct. . . .
> The new masters were growing intolerant of
> criticism but this attitude merely incensed
> the press to intensify their fight against
> corruption, nepotism and tribal jingoism
> which were the bane of the era.

Although my assessment of the press during the civilian rule is obviously at odds with this claim, I am
in agreement with the latter part of the statement.

> The press gave all the support the govern-
> ments needed to make the new military re-
> gime succeed. And it is to the credit of
> the press that in the course of helping the
> FMG to accomplish its onerous task, the
> press has not shirked its responsibilities
> of lambasting the government for some of
> its ineptitudes, excesses and planlessness.
> . . . The press has been stymied by the
> federal government and some editors detained
> for daring to speak the truth or reflect the
> yearnings of the governed.[1]

It could be argued that the press, following an informal and perhaps unconscious review of its impotence
and malperformance during the civilian rule, was
resolved never again to fall into such disrepute.
Thus informal acceptance of the dictum "Publish and
be damned" seemed almost inevitable.

> The editor of the *Nigerian Tribune* was jailed in
> March 1969 when he published an editorial critical of
> the military regime's performance. "It is in the
> interest of the country . . . and of the Nigerian Army
> that we return to civilian rule. Some critics have
> accused some of the military leaders of behaving as if
> they did not want the war to end. Others have said
> that the corrective regime has, in fact, corrected
> nothing. The most immediate answer to these critics
> is an immediate return to civilian government. . . ."[2]

A rash of editorials critical of the military
regime appeared in the middle of 1971. Arrest of
the newspaper editors, in accordance with the detention decree, was not visibly effective as an instrument of deterrence. As the managing editor of the
Daily Times correctly observed, "Almost every editor of
any important newspaper, including those owned by governments, has seen the inside of a police cell or army
orderly room." This was partly because "in the absence
of a democratically elected Parliament, newspapers
found themselves playing the role of a deliberative
assembly reflecting the feelings of the people, their
peccadilloes, their likes and dislikes of government
policies and actions and the conduct of the people who
run the government."[3] The *New Nigerian*, owned by the
northern states, resented the arrest, detentions, and
interrogations of correspondents throughout the federation. It warned the government about the ramifica-
tion of such actions.[4] By and large the journalists
seemed resolved to perform the role that they and many
other Nigerians saw as rightfully theirs. One Nigerian
journalist emphatically declared, "We must examine
those things our leaders should have done that they
didn't do and those things they should not have done
that they did."[5] Even a veteran and highly respected
moderate journalist such as Alhaji Babatunde Jose
declared before a national meeting of the Nigerian
press that journalists must give readers all the news—
social, political, and economic—in spite of the limited freedom of the press under the country's state of
emergency. It is the duty of the press, he said: to
inform readers of what individuals, groups, and government are doing for the peace, progress, and happiness of the state; to criticize irregularities in government; to champion good causes and to right wrongs;
to defend civil liberties; to expose corruption; to
extol the moral values of the people; to preserve
Nigeria as an indivisible nation; and to obey laws of
truth and justice. The strategy of the press should
be "militancy without hostility." He concluded:

> My view is that, in the circumstance of our
> country today, we practitioners of journal-
> ism may regard days, weeks and months behind
> iron bars as professional hazards, we must
> not allow a situation whereby our newspapers,
> radio and television stations will be killed
> for what, in a state of emergency, is regarded
> as excesses but routine in normal circumstances.

> Freedom of the press in a state of emergency
> is a bundle of contradictions and irreconcil-
> ables. Eight years of a state of emergency
> is long enough. And four years after the end
> of our civil war, the peace-loving people of
> Nigeria would be happy to see the abrogation
> of these emergency regulations. I know, of
> course, that some of my views on this subject
> may not be popular among the young generation
> of publish-and-be-hanged journalists and the
> sycophants in the corridors of power.[6]

The Nigerian Guild of Editors, at its February
1975 meeting in Kaduna, deplored what they regarded
the continuous misunderstanding of the role of the
press by officials of the FMG. In the view of the
guild, the proper role of the press is to be the
watchdog of the public, not only to publicize the
problems and achievements of government, but also to
mirror public opinion to the government by commenting
on matters of national interest. The government was
assured, however, that the editors, as patriotic
Nigerians, were mindful of their stake in the peace,
progress, and stability of the country and would take
this into account in the discharge of their function.
While not denying the possibility of a few abuses, the
editors held that the existing laws of sedition and
defamation were more than adequate to check excesses
by the press.[7]

At best the Nigerian press believed that there
was considerable restriction on freedom of expression
in Nigeria, at worst that Nigeria was not a free society but a military dictatorship.[8] It is necessary to
cite and quote these sources in order to show the general disposition of members of the press toward the
military regime. In addition we need to be aware of
the general environment and particularly the constraints
under which the press operated so that we can fully
grasp the conviction of its assessment of government.

The government's unyielding attitude in defiance
of the calls for the abrogation of decrees 21 and 53
as they relate to freedom of the press is an index of
its belief in the influence of the press, even in a
society that remains approximately 65 percent illiterate. The government's perception of the relative
power of the press can also be gleaned from General
Hassan's plea for support. He pointed out that the

press in any society possesses enormous power with
which it could "make or mar" any development effort by
any government. He implored the Nigerian press to
publicize the "achievement of the government in the
direction of national development." Otherwise Nigeria
"would merely be sinking a lot of naira without achieving anything."[9] We may conclude that from the point
of view of members of the press—and objectively from
the point of view of the literate readership's demands
for a free and unfettered press—the Nigerian press
assessment of performance is very important.

In examining the military regime's performance
I have relied heavily upon two major Nigerian newspapers. The *Daily Times* is Africa's largest newspaper
with the widest circulation. Interestingly, it is an
independent, Nigerian-owned newspaper. The *New Nigerian*
is a most influential northern Nigerian newspaper
owned partly by the northern states. It is generally
regarded as conservative. Although opinions from
other newspapers are brought in from time to time,
between these two newspapers a composite and representative picture of the Nigerian press's perception
of government performance emerges. The methodology
here is to let the editorial opinions speak for themselves on the various aspects of government policies
and performance. These opinions are bolstered with
pronouncements of the professional association of
Nigerian journalists.

The bishop of the Anglican diocese of Ibadan in
the Western State called upon the military regime to
devise policies aimed at helping the poor, the weak,
and the unemployed. The *New Nigerian* used the occasion
to comment on government efforts and plans in the area
of social welfare and equity.

> The citizens of this country deserve social
> security measures that will ensure their
> personality development and quality of life.
> Admittedly, this is one of the subjects the
> Udoji Commission is expected to look into in
> an effort to improve conditions of service
> of those employed by the governments and
> statutory corporations. But its work involves
> only a small percentage of the total popula-
> tion of the country. Besides, it is neces-
> sary to plan the old age pension as part of
> a national social security scheme which should

include health schemes, unemployment pension,
etc. Secondly, with the growing individual-
ism and concern for worldly materials in our
generation, the traditional African extended
family system is now under greater stress and
already there are predictions that it can no
longer contain the situation. If this happens, the old, weak and the unemployed would
be left to fend for themselves. The F.M.G.
should therefore not only concern itself with
the economic development of this nation, but
also with spreading the results of economic
development more evenly and widely. It is
therefore to be hoped that in the new development plan, a solid foundation for a comprehensive national social security scheme
will be introduced. The recent oil boom has
provided us with an opportunity to improve,
in real terms, the welfare of the masses.
Economic development without accompanying
social policies to enhance better life for
the citizens of this country does not make
any sense. This is the most opportune time
for action.[10]

On rural development performance the government
received low accolades from the *New Nigerian:* "But living conditions in the rural areas are far from being
satisfactory. Our governments have to double their
effort in providing more essential amenities in the
rural areas. In particular, the provision of water,
shelter and good roads are urgently needed."[11] In
providing housing for the masses the *Daily Times* believed
that government performance was inadequate.

Shelter is one of the basic human needs. And
it should be of great priority in any welfare
programme. Unfortunately, most people in the
country today, particularly the teeming masses in the urban centers, are finding it a
grim battle to meet this basic need. In
Lagos, for instance, up to 10 people squeeze
themselves into a room that is barely sufficient for one. The situation has become so
grave that some people now live in Agege,
Ikorodu and even Badagry from where they
travel daily to their places of work in Lagos.
The less fortunate ones make do with open
spaces under bridges and in recreation gardens,

thereby endangering their health. The situation is not much better in other big towns.
Yet, day after day, houses spring up in our
cities and towns, but there is no room for
the common man. The modern landlord no
longer has the low-income worker in mind as
a prospective tenant: he mainly builds self-
contained flats which only the rich can afford. Worse still, rents on existing room-
and-parlour houses continue to soar in spite
of the much-publicised rent edicts by many
state governments. This was not unexpected,
for efforts to control the price of a commodity for which demand far exceeds supply
are always futile. The only realistic solution, therefore, is for the governments to
provide enough accommodation for the low-
income workers. We have, for long, been
treated to declarations of intention by the
governments on the massive provision of
housing for the low-income workers. In the
past, too, some of the houses built ostensi-
bly for poor workers were eventually occu-
pied by people in the middle and upper classes. The governments must not allow this to
happen again. We admit that the Federal
Government has taken bold and admiral steps
to build houses for workers in all the 12
states. This as well as the bold action of
state governments on housing are also commendable. We however suggest that greater
emphasis be given to the construction of
houses designed to meet the needs of the
low-income group whose problem is clearly
acute. Single bed-room houses with large
living rooms would be ideal for a single
family with is characteristic of an average
Nigerian low-income worker.[12]

The press has been very critical of the performance of the government in the area of agriculture. A
newspaper wanted to know why agriculture had been
doing so poorly. It concluded: "It is high time we
embarked on plantation farming which in other developed countries such as Brazil and Malaysia, which produce virtually the same agricultural export crops as
Nigeria, has proved to be an effective means of achieving increased output."[13] A *Daily Times* editorial expressed little or no confidence in government extension

services and agricultural officers.[14]

All the Nigerian newspapers have called for devising and increasing incentives to farmers. Illustrative of these calls is an editorial urging monetary rewards, adequate storage facilities, the provision of farm machinery for rent, improving the condition of rural women, and ensuring an effective cooperative system.[15] In general Nigerian journalists became skeptical about and critical of the Gowon regime's agricultural policies because of what they believed to be a record of poor performance. For example, the *Daily Times* was critical of government capacity to bring about agricultural revolution because of the poor performance record of its marketing board policy.[16]

In an editorial entitled "Belated Projects" the *New Nigerian* used the permanent secretary of the Ministry of Mines and Power as its whipping boy. It is evident through a close reading of the editorial that the newspaper, like other newspapers, disagreed with the government's priorities and had a low assessment of its performance of self-declared policies. Among other things the editorial said:

> Mr. Asiodu also took it upon himself to defend the indefensible--the recurrent imbalance in sectoral allocation especially the 800 million naira gross expenditure on roads and other related services as compared to the small sums spent on agriculture. And in citing the much talked-about universal primary education, it is absurd to argue that the latter would help the future farmers whose parents have from time immemorial borne the nation's burden, but who until recently have been virtually neglected--nay forsaken, because of a curious admixture of lack of foresight, crooked reasoning and sheer callous indifference. While it is easy to produce watery arguments for the satisfaction of officialdom and bureaucratic promises it is that much harder to convince the audience. Worse still, before the full effects of all these belated but well meaning projects could manifest themselves a lot of damage would have been done and the economic loss incalculable.[17]

In its comment on the government's progress report on agriculture this *Daily Times* editorial conveyed dismay:

> Nor has serious attention been paid to the
> agricultural sector. Somewhere in the re-
> port, it is admitted that there is a case
> for immediate intervention by government to
> arrest the deteriorating situation in the
> production of export crops such as palm oil.
> It is also observed that the states' food
> production programme has not been very suc-
> cessful because of "lack of adequate funds
> for project implementation." Other reasons
> for failure to implement projects indicate
> difficulties in getting feasibility studies
> completed, changes in sectoral priorities,
> infrastructural constraints and the like.
> We can accept some of the reasons. But it
> is obvious that the government cannot justi-
> fiably blame all the shortcomings of the
> plan on lack of funds. Every Nigerian knows
> that funds are available for project imple-
> mentation although only a small portion of
> the total funds allocated to each of the
> sectors has been disbursed. We only hope
> that the lessons of the progress report will
> now be learned as a guide to the Third Plan.[18]

The press was not silent either about the military regime's use of natural resources. Commenting under the heading "Benefits from Nigerian oil" the *Daily Sketch*, owned by the government of the Western State, was critical of the FMG's overall performance, particularly in the areas of equity and agriculture.[19] The *Nigerian Herald*, owned by the Kwara State remained unconvinced. It wondered about the government's capacity to manage its new-found wealth and decried the apparent lack of executive capacity and the seeming failure of government to bring about "equity."[20]

The *New Nigerian* wanted the regime to know that nothing disturbed the ordinary citizen more than infla-tion. It contended that, measured by the volume and intensity of the letters it received and the flow of letters to radio stations in the country, there was no question about the primacy of this concern. The paper profoundly regretted that no one could share the

optimism of the Price Control Board, in view of its
dismal record, to ensure that the Udoji awards would
not compound inflation. The paper suggested other
alternatives to the problem.[21]

   In a 1973 independence anniversary editorial the
Daily Times took an overall inventory of the military
regime's performance. It argued that if peace by
emergency is accepted then politically Nigeria had
continued to enjoy internal peace. Although this may
be misleading, it is a justifiable claim relative to
the situation that existed in the country from 1964 to
1969. In aggregate terms it believed that economic
growth performance may have been substantial. The
government had created special banks for commerce and
agricultural promotion. It had taken substantial
shares in private commercial banks and oil industries.
The *Daily Times* concluded that here the means had been as
laudable as the end. "We indigenize, but with sober
maturity and a high sense of responsibility." But the
Nigerian economy was far from a take-off stage according to the *Times*. "The second national development
plan which should have brought the goal of economic
prosperity much nearer has been a disappointment."
The *Daily Times* hoped that economic modernization would
continue to be kept in view and that every effort
would be made to reach the goal. It concluded
poignantly:

> On the whole our achievements abroad have
> made a much greater impact than our succes-
> ses at home. But we are still far from
> achieving that crucial strength that uplifts
> a nation to greatness. Bribery and corrup-
> tion permeate our society to an incredible
> extent. Our love of money and influence is
> by far higher than our love of country.
> Many of our citizens have no sense of devo-
> tion to duty. We do not yet realise . . .
> that the means by which providence raises a
> nation to greatness are the virtues inspired
> in its men.[22]

   A year after this relative low performance rating
by the *Daily Times,* the *New Nigerian* added its own mixed
review of government development performance and
potential.

   The figures indicating financial resources

> available to the country are absolutely
> staggering: 30,000m naira over the plan
> period means that for each year of the
> 1975-80 plan there is more money available
> than over the whole of the current plan
> which initially envisaged a total expendi-
> ture of ₤1,950 or under 4,000m naira. As
> a broad comment we consider the plan with-
> out seeing the details (which will be pub-
> lished on launching in April) as much too
> ambitious. If we recall that executive
> capacity was a major constraint in the cur-
> rent plan, it is plain that optimism is
> walking on high stilts in the corridors of
> power.[23]

Next the editorial raised the issue of priorities and
expressed serious doubts about the wisdom of conceiv-
ing development in terms of dollars spent or the so-
called performance ratio.[24] This the paper regarded
as a most commendable contribution of the military
regime. It remained unimpressed with the FMG's anticorruption performance, however.

> As of now, the public cannot be sure whether
> the FMG wants to tackle corruption or not,
> because there is such a gap between repeated
> public statements and the stark realities.
> In particular, we caution against using
> "security" as a cover to suppress those who
> might make unpleasant disclosures. The Com-
> mander-in-Chief wants the public to put trust
> in the normal processes of complaint, but it
> is the inability of the system to respond
> which has driven a few desperate people to
> swear affidavits.[25]

It made a very strong plea for a responsive military
regime and rapid but orderly progress toward the rees-
tablishment of a democratic civilian government.[26]

In a 1975 New Year's editorial the *New Nigerian* suggested that the country's resources were not being managed well.

> Oil again has been king. In a real way the
> colossal revenues from mining have helped
> to paper over several cracks in the national
> edifice. Unfortunately the revenues have

apparently convinced the policy makers that
prudence and frugality do not go together
with huge resources. But (as in Libya) they
should. We must learn to go back to proper
methods of expending public funds. Therein
lies the ultimate accountability of any
government.[27]

Two years earlier the *Daily Times* had written:

The fact is that unless this country is very
careful it may find on its hands in the near
future a social problem much more serious
than it can tackle. The time to plan ahead
is now--while our oil wells continue to yield
apparently inexhaustible wealth. Tomorrow
may be too late. Much more serious, the gulf
separating one class of Nigerians from another continues to widen as the rich become
richer and the poor become poorer. The benefits of independence have not been equitably
distributed for the masses remain disinher-
ited and continue to wallow in abject poverty,
while discriminatory fortune continues to
smile only on the lucky few.[28]

A later editorial was more subtle but equally effective in making its point.

With oil flowing at nearly 3 million barrels
per day at more than ₦10 per barrel, no one
could feel greatly surprised that we are now
worth some ₦3 billion in foreign earnings.
In fact experts are already predicting that
we may hit the 5 billion naira mark in no
distant future. What would amaze every
Nigerian is the recent revelation by the
governor of the Central Bank, Dr. Clement
Isong, in a television interview, that managing these earnings poses a problem to this
nation. It is indeed ironical that any
developing nation whose citizens live in
want, ignorance and disease could assume a
posture of affluence by hoarding useful earnings, realizing that their purchasing power
could depreciate substantially overnight.
Only last week the pound got down to its lowest level in history. Dr. Isong himself con-
fessed in the same television interview that

our rural agriculture needs modernisation
in order to produce more food for our consumption. How do we intend to achieve this
without importing machinery, fertilizers and
perhaps expert services in agriculture and
allied fields? Neither is agriculture the
only sector of our economy that can absorb
much of the foreign reserves. The Nigerian
Airways is operating with too few aircraft
to be really effective; the Nigerian Railway
Corporation uses outmoded coaches and en-
gines while the Apapa Wharf is forever
congested. [29]

In 1974 the *Daily Times* began a series of effective
exposés of public corruption. It was by no means the
only newspaper to show its serious intention to help
in the "war against corruption"—all the Nigerian
newspapers joined the campaign. Commenting on the
government performance on anticorruption, which the
government had declared as a major goal, the *New
Nigerian* wrote:

What is of interest at this stage to us is
the steady flow of warning to the judiciary
and the press against allowing themselves
to become the avenues of character assassi-
nation and blackmail. The position of the
government functionaries issuing this warning is understandable. There is the danger
of the two institutions being used to attack
people holding public offices out of ulterior motives. Nevertheless it will be a
dangerous development to even attempt to
force the two institutions to deny access to
people with genuine complaints against public officials who have abused the public
trust to enrich themselves illegally or to
break the country's laws. The judiciary has
the clear duty, among other things, to try
matters brought before it--and to hear affidavits. The press has the duty to inform
and to expose public officers who behave with
impropriety. Neither institution can know
in advance which matter or affidavit is friv-
olous. Either they are free to perform their
duty or they are not. There is no halfway
house. The alternative to this open and democratic system of dialogue is the well-known

phenomenon of anonymous letters. These letters are often the results of frustration
after all other channels of complaints have
been denied to the aggrieved. The recent
experience shows that this alternative can
be a more potent weapon of character assas-
sination and blackmail than the affidavits.
The best way out for all those holding positions of public trust lies in the path of
probity. They should not only uphold the
laws of the country and live within their
legitimate income but should be seen to do
so.[30]

Although allegedly commenting on the Ethiopian military junta the *Daily Times* remarked, "Nothing discredits
a corrective regime faster than for it to prove itself
glaringly corrupt--a sad irony which is easily observ-
able in most of the African countries where the military have secured power."[31]

Newspaper editors were not the only ones critical
of government policies and performance. The Lagos
branch of the Nigerian Union of Journalists made its
views known at an emergency weekend meeting. According to a newspaper account the union was

much concerned about the escalating incidence
of all types of corrupt practices going on in
both high and low places in our society as
evidenced by allegations which have been sur-
facing at an alarming rate in the recent past.
In view of the fact that these allegations
portray the country to the outside world as
a nation of bribe-takers and "ten percenters",
the union called on the Federal Government to
pursue more vigorously its anti-corruption
crusade and to investigate meticulously,
through its law-enforcement agencies, all sur-
facing allegations of corruption, bribe-taking
and abuse of public office no matter the personality involved. The union expressed its
solidarity with Nigerian newspaper editors,
the Newspaper' Proprietors Association and
others who had the rare courage to expose corruption in public life, and gave an assurance
of its unflinching support in this patriotic
endeavor believing as it did that "we must
either swim or sink together". The union

further called on the government not to
encroach on the freedom of the Nigerian
press merely because it was discharging its
sacred duty to help the government in rid-
ding the country of corrupt elements--a
task the government had earlier dedicated
itself to accomplish in its nine-point programme as enunciated by the Head of State,
General Yakubu Gowon. The union called on
all Nigerian journalists not to be brow-
beaten by recent threats to intimidate them
in their anti-corruption battle until vic-
tory was finally won.[32]

Finally, while pretending to address itself to
the issue of academic freedom the *Daily Times* left no
doubt about its sympathy with the generally low performance ratings that the students had given to the
military regime.

We believe it is also wrong to close universities as a means of punishing students for
showing keen interest in the political, social and economic problems of our country.
For, to ask university undergraduates to be
indifferent to the nation's complex problems
or to clap in delight at every solution offered by the authorities for these problems,
is to completely miss the real aim of university education. While vandalism and wanton
destruction of property by students should
be discouraged, the authorities must sympa-
thise with the ardour and hope in our undergraduates' spirit of dissent. We believe
that in a country with so many sycophants
and timid people, it is dangerous to produce
unreflecting graduates whose minds have been
conditioned to comply with evils.[33]

To sum up, let us address ourselves to the specific performance assessment questions raised in
chapter 1. Available evidence indicates that generally
the Nigerian press believed that the government was
doing a tolerable job relative to economic growth.
Yet, expecting great accomplishments from the military
regime because of the oil boom and the resultant increase in revenue, they were very disappointed that
the government's performance had not matched its promise and its potential in all economic sectors,

particularly the agricultural sector.

The press overwhelmingly remained unconvinced that government had succeeded in bringing about equity. Similarly, while not denying increasing concern for social development on the part of the government, the press seemed dissatisfied with the quality, quantity, and rate of progress. As some of the editorials suggest the Nigerian press in many instances was incredulous about government claims and future performance on this score. While there was an admission of relative political stability, the general recognition of the press was that this had been achieved through prohibition of political activities. They seemed to believe that political stability, as defined by the military, is unattainable. There was general agreement that a higher degree of unity was seemingly evident in Nigeria under the military rule.

By self-appointment the Nigerian Press regards itself a primary participant in the system, although the journalists were convinced that the military regime would rather not have them participate. They complained about conscious government attempts to withhold ordinary information from them. They were irked by what they saw as lack of responsiveness to the spokesmen for the interests of ordinary Nigerians.

All Nigerian newspapers made increasing and consistent demands for freedom of the press, freedom of expression, the abrogation of the state of emergency, and the release of all political detainees. This suggests that they remained essentially unconvinced that Nigeria had become a free country. Furthermore, the detention of journalists and the desire of the government to create a Nigerian Press Council without the consent of the Nigerian journalists involved suggest that the press had cause to feel that its interests were not sufficiently represented.

Labor's Perception

Robin Cohen, Robert Nelson, and T. M. Yesufu have all discussed in greater detail the traditional pattern of relationship between the Nigerian government and the labor unions.[34] Each of them has dealt in some way with the history, structure, and problems of Nigerian labor. Of interest here is the perception

of government performance by Nigerian labor. Nonethe-
less, it is necessary to observe that one of the most
damaging weaknesses of the Nigerian labor organizations
is their apparent lack of unity, which handicapped
labor as a successful pressure group. It is noteworthy
that whenever labor has managed to unite it has succeeded in forcing the Nigerian government to satisfy
specific labor interests. A case in point is the success of the Joint Labor Action Committee, initiated in
1963 by the Nigerian Trade Union Congress (NTUC) and
later joined by the United Labour Congress (ULC) and
other groups, with reference to improving working conditions and the success of the subsequent general
strike. The United Front of Labor Organizations before
the Adebo Commission is another. If the attempts of
Nigerian labor to achieve permanent unity should succeed—and the chances look good—then their perception
of the nature and quality of performance of the regime
could be critical.

The military seemed to have recognized the importance of labor as well as its own vulnerability to
industrial action when it introduced Decree 21 of 1968
and Decree 53 of 1969.[35] Various demands for abrogation of these decrees were ignored. Decree 21 severely
curtailed the right to strike and Decree 53 totally
abolished that right. According to the decree:

1. It is an offense to publish in newspaper,
   radio, or television or by any other means
   of mass communication anything which could
   cause public alarm or industrial unrest.
   Thus, it is a criminal offense to carry news
   of public strikes or lock-outs.

2. The inspector general of police and the
   chief of staff of the armed forces are
   granted the right of arbitrary detention.

3. The writ of habeas corpus, the instrument
   for challenging unlawful detention is sus-
   pended. Thus the arresting officers cannot be questioned.

Even with these decrees there was an increase in industrial action, particularly as the Nigerian civil war
progressed.[36]

One clear index of lack of confidence in the

government's interest in the Nigerian worker is the workers' reaction to the Udoji recommendations. In chapter 2 the intention of the Udoji Report and the numerous and intense industrial actions that followed this award were discussed. The government was shocked by the reaction of labor and claimed that "the honest attempts of government to better the lots of its workers are being deliberately misinterpreted.[37]

The reaction of the workers and their refusal to follow the prescribed procedure to seek redress represents a general but succinct lack of confidence in government institutions for wage review and the workers' opinion that, left to itself, the government would not protect the interests of the working class. Amazingly enough, it was not only the so-called traditional working class that took to demonstrations and strikes—teachers, bankers, and doctors joined in. Throughout January 1975 there were hundreds of strikes, and the economy could have been paralyzed except for the diplomacy of the newly appointed commissioner of labor.[38]

The national vice-president of the ULC, Alhaji Abubakar Abutu, asked the FMG to scrap the Price Control Board because of what he termed an "indifferent attitude to the unprecedented jump in the prices of commodities."[39] As pointed out in chapter 2, the board was viewed as an important institution designed to prevent the exploitation of the masses. Worker dissatisfaction with the organization was a serious indictment of government performance. The assistant general secretary of the ULC was more direct. "It is a pity that the so-called Price Control Board controls nothing, rather the Board has been causing confusion." His solution to the problem of food scarcity is quite interesting: establishment of agricultural farms in all states and the utilization of soldiers on these farms.

The Nigerian Workers Council, one of four central labor organizations, called upon the FMG to tackle and solve the problem of inflation and the acute shortage of essential commodities in Nigeria.[40] Furthermore, Mr. Akpan, the secretary of the steering committee of the Nigerian Labour Congress, believed that it is untenable to argue that a shortage or absence of essential commodities was due to congestion at the ports. He submitted that a military regime should be able to

tackle such problems with military precision in order
to ensure the availability of such goods. The implication is quite clear; the government rationale of
port congestion, even if true, reflects poor performance. The labor rating of the government's economic
performance appears to be low.

The labor leaders consistently stated their objection to government's failure to consult with labor.
They warned: "We do not want to be taken for granted.
We find it difficult to carry government messages to
the workers about a programme which we never partici-
pated in planning."[41]

Some of the demands put forward by the spokesman
for the Western State Workers before the Adebo Committee indicate that in 1971 the workers did not believe that the military government had performed excep-
tionally well. Here are some of the items:

> In our bid to build an egalitarian society,
> the Nigerian worker, his union should be
> treated as essential arms of economic power
> and their support at all times for social,
> political and economic schemes must be sought.
> It is through their involvement in the scheme
> of things that any wage increase now or in
> the future could have any value to the Nigerian
> peasants, cooperators, petty-traders and the
> workers. In conclusion, Mr. Chairman, your
> Commission should examine the following sug-
> gestions in light of our experiences:
>
> (a) a new policy to ensure workers participa-
>   tion in management at all levels, includ-
>   ing top policy making bodies;
>
> (b) the abrogation of Trade Disputes Emer-
>   gency Provisions Decree No. 53 of 1969;
>
> (c) removing all control of State Owned
>   Companies and Statutory Corporations by
>   top government bureaucrats who possess
>   no knowledge of modern business methods;
>
> (d) the retraining of our civil servants
>   especially the "old horses" promised in
>   the country's four year economic blue-
>   print should commence immediately;

(e) ensuring better understanding between
the Federal Military Government and the
Nigerian Labour Movement through closer
contacts, representation on Committees,
Commission, Local, State and National
Government;

(f) the creation of state mechanised farms
throughout the country to be manned by
those hands now at rest since the end
of hostilities. This will help the production of more foodstuffs and finished
food products;

(g) the rent and price control scheme being
pursued by various governments in the
Federation are commendable but it is
the production of more foodstuffs and
building of more low cost housing that
can help the situation;

(h) the Federal Military Government should
halt the present exploitation of our
resources by foreigners especially in
the oil, industrial, and agricultural
sectors. It should either be in partnership with well organised Nigerian business men or government. No foreigner
should be allowed to go it alone anymore.[42]

These demands clearly indicate that until 1972 these
workers did not believe that they were adequately represented in the councils of government. Nor were they
satisfied that their interests were being adequately
protected and serviced. Moreover, one detects a certain lack of confidence in the government bureaucracy
as it was then constituted, and there is a subtle hint
that the military should be made to contribute directly
to the economic production of society. Finally, they
left no doubt that the goal of equity had not been
achieved.

The general view of labor was that the military
regime was itself corrupt. Thus, we find Mr. Goodluck,
the general secretary of the Nigerian Trade Union Federation calling on the military regime to set up a
high-powered tribunal to examine assets of all public
officials including the armed forces.[43] At Ibadan,
the Sketch Technical and General Workers Union demanded

to know government policy on the expected role of the
company "in promoting understanding between the government and the governed as well as in the crusade
against social vices which the military administration
had made an avowed duty to wipe out."[44]

Even as early as 1968 the NTUC, while generally
supportive of the regime's territorial integrity policies, had started to take sharp barbs at its development performance.

> Cheaper transportation is yet a dream. I am
> not unmindful of the titanic task of the Fed-
> eral Military Government, yet the non-
> implementation of the housing scheme cannot
> be defended. . . . The NTUC has carefully
> studied recent economic measures and wishes
> to give its full support to a policy which
> it regards as noble and patriotic. However
> the Congress wishes to express its misgiving
> in what it believes to be an "Economic Mirage
> Mission."[45]

According to a 1969 survey taken from a sample of university workers, 93 percent agreed that labor was not
getting a fair share of the country's resources. Only
26 percent of those interviewed said that they trusted
the Nigerian army officers.[46]

The pronouncements of labor leaders after 1972 as
well as their reactions to the Udoji Report indicate
that the military regime continued to have a credibility gap with the workers. Unless government performance relative to equity could be demonstrated to the
Nigerian workers, labor alienation and disaffection
were bound to increase. The ramifications of this for
economic productivity and political stability are
self-evident.

CHAPTER FIVE

Perception of Development Performance:
the Military Regime

On the issue of national unity, surprisingly, the military regime's perception of its performance could be interpreted as low. In a speech announcing and justifying the decision not to return power to the civilians in 1976, Gowon admitted failure in this crucial area of national unity.

> In spite of the existence of a state of
> emergency which has so far precluded polit-
> ical activity, there have already emerged
> such a high degree of sectional politick-
> ing, intemperate utterances and writings
> which were deliberately designed to whip
> up ill feelings within the country to the
> benefit of the political aspirations of a
> few. There is no doubt that it would not
> take them long to return to the old cut-
> throat politics that once led this nation
> into serious crisis. We are convinced that
> this is not what the honest people of this
> country want. What the country and the or-
> dinary citizen want is peace and stability,
> the only condition under which progress and
> development are possible.[1]

Whether or not the regime realized it this statement is a direct admission that its efforts to bring about unity in Nigeria—although they may have been sincere— had not succeeded. At best the success was more apparent than real. Assuming that the reason given for the abnegation of its 1976 civilian-rule promise represented its sincere perceptions, the regime's judgment was that its performance on national unity and political stability could not stand the crucial test. The continued existence of the state of emergency despite the demands for its abrogation by virtually

every group in Nigeria (judiciary, students, journalists, labor, lecturers) suggests that the military
regime viewed political stability—if it existed at
all in Nigeria—as very tenuous and fragile. The military governor of Kwara State suggested in a television
interview that those who were demanding the abrogation
of the emergency decree had something up their sleeves.[2]
In this regard Professor Dudley's assessment is curiously and paradoxically in line with that of the military leadership, although both arrive at this conclusion from differing and opposing arguments. Dudley
argues:

> If the civil regime had succeeded in passing
> the preventive detention act it once pro-
> posed, and had behind it an armed force of
> 250,000 men, it also would have been stable.
> To conclude from the absence of opposition
> when there is a state of emergency, when a
> major in the Armed Forces can legally cause
> any citizen to be detained, that a regime is
> stable is not only to misuse language, it is
> also to abuse language.[3]

While the state governors tended to exaggerate
high performance assessments, FMG estimations of performance were generally mixed. On balance its progress report, which was discussed in chapter 2, seems
to give relatively high overall marks to the government's economic performance while noting many shortcomings. The low-performance sectors, according to
the military government, were agriculture and manufacturing. The report noted that in many areas "executive capacity" remained problematic. The federal government's summation of its economic performance concluded:

> It is clear from this report that not only
> has the economy completely recovered from
> the shocks and stresses of the civil war but
> it has continued to maintain a high rate of
> growth. The growth rates of gross national
> product for the first three years exceeded
> the plan targets by 4.9 percent, 6.2 percent
> and 0.7 percent respectively. Most of the
> other economic indicators including capital
> formation, overall exports, balance of pay-
> ments, gross national savings, government
> revenues and expenditures show a much more

remarkable performance than the Plan expected. . . . The resources picture is reasonably good especially for 1971-72 and
1973-74 when actual capital receipts overshot the plan targets by 58% and 62% respec-
tively. The disbursement of external financial assistance has lagged behind expectations but some domestic resources have shown
some buoyancy. The low level of external
resource inflow was not due to lack of adequate foreign loan proposals but rather to
the slow rate of disbursement of negotiated
and committed aid, particularly project aid.
. . . It is important to remark that the
rosy picture painted in this report is
largely due to the rapidly growing mining
sector of the economy. This sector accounts
for about half the growth rate recorded, accounts for large increases in government revenue, is responsible for the much improved
foreign exchange situation, and contributes
substantially to capital formation. The traditional sectors have not done as well. One
is particularly concerned with the performance cultivation of large tracts of land in
the war-affected areas. There is therefore
less room for flow than ever. There is an
urgent need for a bold approach to give a new
lease of life to agriculture while promoting
industrial development. The long-run growth
of the economy will to a large extent depend
on what happens in these two sectors.[4]

The Nigerian head of state spoke more glowingly
of his regime's development performance in October
1974. Relevant excerpts from Gowon's 1974 progress
report to the nation follow. They represent the most
direct evidence of the regime's perception of specific
and significant achievement.

The main preoccupation of the Second Plan
was to rehabilitate and reconstruct the
wreckage of the civil war and hopefully to
achieve progress and even development for
the rest of the country. As clearly indicated in the second progress report published a few months ago, the national economy, between 1970 and 1974, performed much
better than expected. The growth rate of

the national income during the period has
been well over 10 per cent even when allowance has been made for inflationary increases
in the general level of prices. In terms of
actual capital expenditure on development
projects, the governments of the federation
have spent a total of about ₦2,200 million
since the Second Plan was launched in November, 1970. All things considered, this has
been a satisfactory performance. I now wish
to direct attention to the developments which
have taken place in the vital sectors of the
national economy.

In agriculture, most of the farms and plantations abandoned during the civil war have
been rehabilitated and brought back into production. Furthermore, in recognition of the
vital importance of the agriculture in the
nation's economy, government has intensified
its extension service efforts and increased
the supply of fertilizers and other requirements, to the farmers. To this end, capital
expenditure of about ₦230 million was made
between 1970 and 1974. The marketing board
system has been reformed, and I am happy to
announce that following the approval of the
reform measures by the Supreme Military
Council, producer prices of all agricultural
produce have risen, in several cases by about
100 percent in the last two years. In addition, the Nigerian Agricultural Bank was
effectively established early in 1973, and
during its first year of operation, it gave
about ₦10 million in loans to farmers and
farmers' cooperatives throughout the country.
The efforts of government in the development
of agriculture has however not been limited
to providing assistance to the farmers. In
order to ensure that the nation is able to
feed itself, various governments in the federation have established food production
companies.

In the mining sector the major development
during the Second Plan Period has been the
dominant role which government is now playing by effectively participating in the op-
erations of oil-producing companies. It

may not be generally known that the Federal
Government is now the majority share-holder
in all the foreign oil companies in the country. In addition to its substantial equity
participation in the industry, the Federal
Government established early in 1972 the
Nigerian National Oil Corporation which is
now prospecting for oil in a number of loca-
tions, both on-shore and off-shore. It is
the intention to ensure that through these
and other efforts, Nigerians will in the
near future acquire the technical know-how
required for running the oil industry, from
prospecting and production all the way down
to refining, transportation and distribution.
During the same period, the Nigerian Mining
Corporation was set up by law and charged
with the responsibility of identifying, prov-
ing and mining all solid minerals with the
exception of coal for which a separate corporation already exists. Thus, in this sector, we have established a solid foundation
on which future development schemes will be
based.

The first major problem that faced the manufacturing sector at the beginning of the Second Plan was that of reconstructing the industrial establishments which were damaged during the civil war. By the middle of the
Second Plan Period practically all manufacturing concerns had been reactivated. For
example, the three cement factories in the
war-affected areas, especially those of
Nkalagu and Calabar had not only been brought
back into production, but are now undergoing
substantial expansion. As in the other sectors activities in the manufacturing sector
during the Second Plan Period have not been
limited to the reconstruction of the war-
damaged industries. If I may call attention
to only the major projects in which the Federal Government is directly involved: the
two salt refineries at Ijoko and Sapele will
go into production in the next six months.
Before the middle of next year motor cars
assembled at the Volkswagen and Peugeot assembly plants in Lagos and Kaduna will be available on the Nigerian market. Substantial

progress has also been made on the implementation of the Second Oil Refinery at Warri.
The Kaduna single super phosphate fertilizer
project is now under construction while the
Nitrogenous Fertilizer and the Petrochemical
Complex are both at final decision stages.
As regards the iron and steel project which
featured in our First and Second National
Development Plans, the intensive geological
work undertaken during the Second Plan Period
has led to the discovery of high quality iron
ore. A decision has therefore been made on
both the location of the project and the process to be adopted. If we are able to keep
to the present implementation schedule, we
should be producing iron and steel in Nigeria
by 1980. During the Second National Development Plan Period the Nigerian Enterprises
Promotions Decree was promulgated to give
Nigerians the opportunity to own completely,
or in part, important businesses. The promulgation of the decree was a landmark in
the economic history of the country and the
implementation of the decree in spite of the
misgivings and even scepticism at home and
abroad was successful beyond expectations. In
order to further promote general development in commerce and industry, the Nigerian
Bank for Commerce and Industry was established.

One of the most important developments in
education during the Second Development Plan
period was the constitutional amendment which
transferred higher education from the Concurrent Legislative List to the Exclusive Federal
List. Other levels of education were also
put on the concurrent list. Following this
and other changes, the capital allocation to
the education sector rose to over ₦360 million, about half of which had been disbursed
by early last year.

Physical achievements in education are best
illustrated with significant increases in
enrollment at the different levels of the
educational system. The total enrollment in
primary schools rose from 3,500,000 in 1970
to about 4,500,000 in 1973. At the secondary school level, various institutions were

established. These include 12 Federal Government Colleges for boys and 12 colleges
for girls. The Federal Science School was
established on its permanent site while Federal Schools of Arts and Science have just
opened in Mubi, Ogoja and Sokoto.

In the area of technical education, four new
Colleges of Technology and nine Trade Centers
were established by the state governments.
Over the same period, university enrollment
rose to well over 20,000 at the present time.

The head of state concluded:

Other notable achievements during the period
under review include indigenous participation to not less than 40 per cent in the three
leading expatriate-owned commercial banks, the
strengthening of the indigenously owned commercial banks, the introduction of uniform
prices for petroleum products throughout the
federation, the introduction of uniform income tax, the conversion to decimal currency
and the metric system, the changeover to
right hand drive, the completion of the
National Stadium in time for the Second All-
Africa Games in 1973 and the substantial progress made in the construction of the National
Theatre Complex. Some of these are achievements involving delicate negotiations with
powerful foreign interests, requiring a speed
of action and courage on the part of the Federal Government. That the Federal Government
has been able to make the necessary decisions
and conclude the negotiations . . . does
credit not only to our negotiators but also
to the realism and good sense of the foreign
interests concerned.

We must accept, nevertheless, that there have
been areas in which progress has not been as
fast as had been envisaged. We have learnt
valuable lessons in such areas and these lessons will be brought to bear in the implementation of the Third National Development Plan.[5]

The military regime believed that compared to
other countries, including the industrialized world,

the Nigerian economy was doing remarkably well. "This
nation is, today, in the happy and uncommon position
of having a currency that has become very strong. Our
Naira has, of recent, appreciated in relation to the
major trading currencies, namely, the U. S. dollar,
the pound sterling, the yen and the lira. The Federal
Military Government will continue to pursue an active
exchange rate policy to reflect the strength of the
country's balance of payment, with a view to reducing
the degree of imported inflation."[6]

Brigadier Ogbemudia, the Mid-Western governor,
castigated "Nigerian politicans" for clamoring for a
"return to civilian rule without giving due consideration to its implication for Nigerian development."[7]
He said that people are interested only in whether or
not their rulers can provide social amenities and promote economic development, but what is important is
the primacy of the economy and increasing the living
standard of the broad masses of the people. In this
area, he said, the military had out-performed the
politicians.[8]

Unlike some of his military governors the head of
state refrained from directly stating that the military regime's economic and development performances
far outstripped what civilian regimes with the same
resources would have done. He seemed to imply, however, that given their apparent ability to manage
economic growth the military regime was the one most
capable of leading Nigeria in the circumstances. In
short, while a civilian regime might have been able to
do as good a job, or even a better job, with the economy, the military apparently saw a civilian regime as
ill-equipped to cope with the system's predisposition
toward political instability.[9]

The military regime generally remained baffled at
the mounting criticisms leveled against its equity
performance (development). Part of the reason (it has
been discussed fully in chapter 2) is the government's
assumption that plans would work out exactly as laid
out in its blueprint. A case in point is the so-called
Indigenisation Decree, which was criticized for creating a handful of Nigerian millionaires while the lot
of the masses remained essentially untouched.[10] The
frustration of the head of state was dramatically demonstrated when he lamented that the people of Nigeria
did not appreciate the efforts made by the government

to improve their lot. He was venting his disgust at
the wave of demonstrations and criticisms that greeted
the Udoji Wage Report.

At times the military regime appears to have mis-
judged the degree of its support. The FMG believed
that it had the confidence and support of the indigenous businessman.

> In the field of Banking, Commercial Banks
> were able to channel an increasing propor-
> tion of their loans to the more productive
> sectors of the economy, so that 51% of the
> aggregate bank loans went into the more pro-
> ductive sectors in 1974-75. The year 1974-
> 75 thus became the year when, for the first
> time, commercial bank loans and advances to
> the more productive sectors accounted for
> more than half the total banks' loans and
> advances. Also, during the period, the banks
> were able to increase significantly their
> loans and support for indigenous enterprises.
> Expatriate as well as indigenous banks were
> able to exceed the minimum of 40% of their
> total loans and advances which they were di-
> rected to allocate to indigenous business
> enterprises. This is a creditable perform-
> ance as it indicates, not only the growing
> confidence of the banking community in the
> indigenous businessman, but also the sup-
> port of that community for Government Pol-
> icy. With minor modifications, therefore,
> the credit guidelines for 1975-76 will fol-
> low the current pattern.[11]

Although this may have been true of the Nigerian "big
businessmen" it was by no means true of the petty
traders.

In general the military regime assumed that those
who voice objection to government policies and performance are either misinformed, misguided, or inno-
cent victims of the machinations of the ambitious few.
In chapter 3 I discussed the government's perception
of student criticisms. To press criticism the inspector general of police and member of the Supreme Military Council (SMC) and Federal Executive Council (FEC)
replied:

The press has recently mounted a campaign
against the Federal Government pressuring
it to institute an enquiry into the conduct of certain government functionaries
and leveling accusations against individuals who are not in a position to seek legal
remedy. Publishing inciting articles, books
and pamphlets capable of whipping up sectional sentiments or disrupting law and
order have become the order of the day.

This is nothing short of blackmail. The
government would not allow itself to be
blackmailed by the press or stampeded into
taking any action in any matter of public
interest. Malicious press attack on the
government cannot solve any problem. It
is quite obvious that some actions of the
press are clearly designed to cause unrest
in the country. No responsible and patriotic Nigerian would like to see this country
plunged into another crisis. The Federal
Government will no longer tolerate press
indiscipline and calculated attempt to
undermine its authority and government may
be forced to take drastic and unpleasant
measures to curb the excesses of the press.
The police, who have been unjustly accused
of arbitrary arrests of journalists, will
continue to take appropriate action against
offenders and nothing will deter them from
carrying out their legitimate duty of main-
taining law and order.[12]

Major General Hassan Katsina, also a member of
the SMC and the FEC, declared that the duty of the
press is only to inform people about government policies. Various other military governors, including
those of the Rivers, North-Central, and North-Western
states, echoed the same sentiment. There were, of
course, a few exceptions. For example, Major General
Ekpo insisted that Nigeria was not a police state and
that freedom of expression on any matter should not be
curtailed. Brigadier Rotimi said that he backed freedom of the press without condition, telling the press,
"You must be prepared to face all odds."[13]

This perception of the military regarding its

performance, and the assessment of others about its
rule, is important because a regime can develop, uncon-
sciously, a "persecution complex," which could only
harden the regime. If one imputes ulterior motivations
to a relatively open, critical expression of performance, the quality, quantity, and effect of feedback
may be seriously endangered.

At times the military's assessment of its overall
support reflected a very selective perception. Consider the following statement justifying the government decision to stay in power beyond 1976:

> Understandably, therefore, a large number of
> well-meaning and responsible Nigerians from
> all walks of life and from all parts of the
> country as well as well-wishers of Nigeria at
> home and abroad have called attention to the
> lack of wisdom and the danger inherent in ad-
> hering to the target date previously announced.
>
> Our own assessment of the situation as of now
> is that it will be utterly irresponsible to
> leave the nation in the lurch by a precipitate
> withdrawal which will certainly throw the nation
> back into confusion.[14]

The data in chapters 3 and 4 indicate that this was in
fact contrary to the wish of the majority of Nigerians.
Many members of the military as late as July 1974 also
expressed opposition to a continuation of military rule
beyond 1976. Among these were Major General Ekpo,
Brigadier Esuene, and Brigadier Johnson.[15] Johnson
was quoted as saying that he would resign unless the
promise were kept. Brigadier Rotimi, while addressing
himself to military rule and performance, said:

> All this is not to advocate that the military
> is at all times a better alternative form of
> government which should be perpetuated. Some-
> thing may be said for dictatorships, in peri-
> ods of storm and turbulence; but in these
> cases the dictator rises in true relation to
> the whole moving throng of events. He rides
> the whirlwind because he is a part of it.
> He is the monstrous child of emergency. He
> may well possess the force and quality to
> dominate the minds of millions and sway the
> course of history. Nonetheless, he should

pass with the crises. To make a permanent
system of dictatorship, either through military intervention or any other device, is
to prepare the ground for a new cataclysm.
Happily for Nigeria, there is no cause for
anxiety as the military has announced its
intention to retire in 1976.[16]

On the other hand, Brigadier Jallo and Colonel Bajowa
went on record as opposing the return to civilian rule.
Bajowa said, "It is better in the overall interest of
this country that the military stays three or four
more years, if necessary, for peace rather than to
just lay hands off in 1976 in chaos because it does
not want to be accused of lust for power."[17] Brigadier
Jallo went further: he wanted ten more years.[18]

On balance the military regime believed it had
advanced economic growth and development satisfactorily. It recognized some problem areas but remained
optimistic that its performance rating would be high.
Although not quite sure about its level of support, it
seemed confident that it could achieve its overall
goals through a combination of coercion, high economic
performance, and occasional co-optation. It wavered
between an apparent unwillingness to recognize the
accuracy of the low ratings that significant sectors
had increasingly been awarding the regime and a lack
of self-confidence in the quantity and quality of its
own performance. The government's imputation of evil
motivation to its critics, as well as other evidence,
suggests that the military posture was predominantly
the former. Nevertheless, there were occasional indi-
cations of a painful awareness of failure. In the
words of General Gowon:

> One of the major problems that continues in-
> creasingly to bedevil our economy, is infla-
> tion. . . . In the last three years, each suc-
> cessive budget has attempted to find a solution
> to the problem of inflation or at least tried
> to mitigate its adverse effects. Our problem
> of inflation has been accentuated by the recent
> salaries and wage increases. In addition, the
> enormous investment expenditures which will be
> incurred in both the public and private sector
> during the next five years are likely to have
> inflationary effects which will have to be
> carefully watched in the coming years.[19]

CHAPTER SIX

Conclusion

In chapter 1 three vantage points for development performance assessment were identified: the consumers,
the military government, and the objective data. Chapters 3 and 4 covered the rating by the consumers--
farmers, traders, journalists, students, labor, and
lecturers. The overall picture that emerges is one of
poor development ratings and instances of fair economic
growth performance.[1] Chapter 5 and parts of chapter 2
are concerned with the military government's view of
its performance. The military rulers saw their government as progressing satisfactorily with regard to
both economic growth and development, but they were
not unaware of some glaring pitfalls and the need for
improvement. In parts of chapter 2 the extent of economic growth and development was examined objectively
and in statistical terms. The statistics show that
economic growth performance had generally been satisfactory but that development, as that was defined, had
not been very satisfactory. The reasons for the latter were also discussed. This last chapter is an attempt to restore some balance with an overview of the
present, past, and future of development in Nigeria
under the military regime.

Notwithstanding the low performance ratings detailed in chapter 3, the government was not unrecep-
tive to ideas and suggestions of change. On March 29,
1975 the head of state unfolded his 1975/76 budget
plan, in which it was evident that the government had
adopted some of the suggestions advocated by students,
farmers, workers, and journalists. For example, on
inflation General Gowon asserted:

> Government recognizes fully the crucial
> role which the private sector has to play
> as the main supplier of consumer goods and
> services. It is extremely important that

there should be an adequate supply of con
sumer goods to supplement domestic supply.
Consequently, it has become increasingly
imperative to use import duty relief to encourage the importation of all consumer goods
that are in short supply, subject only to the
need to protect and further develop local industries and agriculture. Government is ever-
conscious of the need to provide import relief,
while at the same time, offering protection
to local industries. Changes have, therefore,
been made in customs and excise duties in a
manner designed to facilitate the importation
of much needed consumer goods to stabilise
the cost of local products, and to create incentive for new local production. Care has
been taken to ensure that the level of duties
on imported inputs by local industries is not
so low as to discourage their local production. Reliefs for local industries have,
therefore, concentrated on reductions in excise duties and company tax.

The main highlights of the tariff changes are
the reduction of import duties on building
materials which are in short supply, from
50% to a maximum of 20%; the reduction of import duties on food items such as salt, rice,
tomatoes, fish and meat generally to 10%.
Import duty on milk has been abolished, while
import duties on general consumer goods, such
as electronics, lanterns and photographic
equipment have been reduced to levels from 5%
to 40%. In view of the growing shortage, the
import duty on beer has been reduced as well.[2]

Seemingly reacting to the disaffection of farmers
and related workers, the government abolished the age-
old cattle tax, hoping that this would bring some much-
needed relief to the cattle owner and encourage him to
keep his cattle within the country.[3] More significantly the government increased producer prices on
perennial crops.[4]

It is also interesting that the government, in
order to encourage further investment in housing development, increased by 50 percent the capital allowance as well as the annual allowance for building
expenditure. Moreover, "the importation of stockfish

which has hitherto been subject to licence, will hence-
forth be removed from licence so as to meet the increased demand in the very sensitive area of food supply. Similarly, the ban on corned beef, edible nuts,
margarine, imitation lard and other prepared edible
fats, have been lifted." In order to ensure real increase in the purchasing power of workers, "the Federal Military Government has approved that 50% of the
arrears of salaries paid to employees in the private
sector by their employers, following the recent salaries agreed between them, should be tax free as was
the case with public servants."[5] The government also
altered the level and pattern of company taxation. If
the companies passed this on to the consumers it would
be helpful, but past experience indicates that this is
unlikely. In any case the small indigenous businessman found that the first ₦6,000 profit of his company
was tax free.

The structural rearrangement of government bureaucracy was especially notable because of the new
industries created: Ministry of Cooperatives and Supply; Ministry of Social Development, Youth, and Sports;
Ministry of Urban Development and Housing and Environment; Ministry of Water Resources; Ministry of Petroleum and Energy; and Ministry of Aviation.[6] All the
new ministries, with the possible exception of Aviation,
had a direct bearing on economic development and equity.
Of course the lack of executive capacity could mili-
tate against what may well have been a significant
structural readjustment that could improve government's
delivery system and overall output.

It must have been disappointing to many Nigerians
who believed that the army was not involved in direct
economic productivity to note that in the 1975/76 budget defense still received a rather high capital expenditure allocation and that agriculture ranked next to
the last. The hierarchy for allocation of 1975/76
federal capital expenditure was as follows:[7]

    ₦1 billion for land transport
    ₦779 million for manufacturing and craft
    ₦736 million for defense
    ₦462 million for education
    ₦423 million for housing
    ₦323 million for communication
    ₦132 million for administration
    ₦171 million for agriculture and meteorology

The only questionable priority may be defense. Judging from the reactions of various groups in the society discussed earlier, an exchange of defense's rank
with agriculture's would have been most welcomed in
this 1975/76 budget. It should be pointed out that
these data do not include statutory and nonstatutory
allocation of revenue to the states. These state
resource allocations could add to any sectoral allocation, with the exception only of defense, an exclusive
concern of the FMG. Taken in this light the Federal
expenditure for defense is not as high as it might
otherwise seem. According to *The Military Balance, 1974-75,*
Nigerian defense spending as a percentage of GNP declined from 13.7 percent to 7.2 percent between 1970
and 1972. Even if this figure is accurate, it is still
rather high compared to the United States (6.4 percent),
but it is lower than Egypt (20.2 percent) and Saudi
Arabia (17.9 percent).[8]

The rude interruption of the Nigerian civil war
three years before the end of the development plan for
the 1962-68 period makes a comparison of performance
during both plan periods very difficult and perhaps
meaningless. The civil war changed the very nature
and style of political leadership, played havoc with
expenditure priorities, and affected the resources and
revenue of the government. All that can be produc-
tively done by way of comparison is to look at government priorities as evidenced by the amount of investment in each sector. Even this is subject to serious
handicaps given the impact of the civil war on the
size, requirements, and maintenance of the Nigerian
armed forces.

An examination of the 1962-68 development plan
indicates that, judging from capital expenditure estimates, government priority, from high to low, was:
1) transport, 2) electricity, 3) primary production
(agriculture), 4) trade and industry, 5) education,
6) general administration, 7) town and country planning, 8) defense, 9) water and sewage, 10) health, and
11) labor and social welfare (see table 19, page 123).
On the other hand, estimated capital revenue allocations for the 1970-74 period reveals this order of
priorities (high to low): 1) transport, 2) defense,
3) education, 4) agriculture, 5) administration,
6) industry, 7) water and sewage, 8) health, 9) information, 10) town and country planning, 11) labor and
social welfare, 12) mining (see table 20, page 123).

TABLE 19
1962-68 Revenue Allocation

Transport	£N 143.817 million
Primary Production (Agriculture)	£N 91.9 million
Industry	£N 90.269 million
Education	£N 69.763 million
Administration	£N 48.089 million
Town and Country Planning	£N 41.746 million
Defense and Security	£N 40.5 million
Water and Sewage	£N 24.258 million
Health	£N 17.076 million
Labor	£N 8.662 million
Information	£N 3.662 million

Source: Nigeria, Federal Ministry of Economic Development and Reconstruction, Central Planning Committee, *National Development Plan 1962-68*, and, *Second National Development Plan 1970-74*.

TABLE 20
1970-74 Capital Expenditure Allocation (Revised)

Transport	₦885,563,377
Defense and Security	₦346,183,211
Education	₦363,232,221
Agriculture	₦304,972,000
Administration	₦266,581,102
Industry	₦162,660,487
Water and Sewage	₦148,676,183
Health	₦138,755,715
Information	₦ 85,318,717
Town and Country Planning	₦ 59,078,910
Labor and Social Welfare	₦ 45,089,131
Mining	₦ 36,661,420

Source: *Second Progress Report.*

TABLE 21
1976-80 Outline of Capital Estimates

Armed Forces	₦2,200 million
Education	₦2,000 million
Agriculture	₦1,400 million
Administration	₦ 854 million
Health	₦ 659 million

Source: *Daily Times*, October 2, 1974, p. 1.

The only notable change was defense, which made a
dramatic shift from eighth in the 1962-68 plan to
second in the 1970-74 plan. It is important to observe, however, that the 1976-80 development plan (see
table 21, page 123) shows marked narrowing of the gap
between defense and other allocations. As indicated
earlier, defense was an exclusive federal item, and
when the 1976-80 estimated allocations for all the
states are combined the total allocation for agriculture exceeds that for defense and security.[9]

The GDP growth rate during the civilian years of
the plan for 1963 through 1966 were 6.7 percent, 3.8
percent, 5.7 percent, and 4.2 percent. Quite apart
from the image of unsteady expansion, the average
annual growth was 5.1 percent. This was half the
annual growth rate of the 1970-74 period. Parenthetically, it should be observed that the projected growth
rate for the second development plan, which was 6.6
percent, was surpassed.

While aggregate growth rate is important, sectoral
rates can tell us more. Consider the 1971-72 figures,
for example. Of the 12 percent overall growth rate
recorded during the year 50% was due to oil. Agriculture netted a poor 2 percent and manufacturing experienced a minimal 1.2 percent growth. The dominance of
oil is evidenced by the decline or minimal increase in
traditional export commodities at the same time that
crude oil export increased in value by nearly 400 percent.[10]   In this respect the Nigerian critics of the
regime experienced a déjà vu: a replacement of the
cocoa monocrop with an oil monocrop. The military
regime appeared conscious of the need to rectify these
deficiencies.

During the four-year period of the second development plan the sectors that experienced the highest
increase were: mining and quarrying (247 percent) and
building and construction (215 percent). The areas
of lowest increases were transport and communications
(48.7 percent), agriculture, livestock, forestry, and
fishing (51.6 percent), and manufacturing and crafts
(71.5 percent).[11]   In the opinion of a Nigerian eco-
nomics expert, Nigeria showed "an economy whose growth
has been highly lopsided, which is heavily dependent
on one product, oil, and in which the contribution of
a very critical sector, manufacturing, has fallen
rather than increased during the Second National
Development Plan period."[12]

A few points of comparison on some sectoral performance follow. During the civilian regime agricultural exports were about 80 percent to 85 percent of
total exports and represented approximately 60 percent
of the GDP.[13] Since some products from the rural sector never reach the market, this figure may have been
underestimated. But agricultural growth during the
1962-68 period did not increase by more than 2 percent
per annum. The GNP agricultural contribution dropped
from 60 percent in the very early 1960s to 53 percent
during the 1962-68 plan period.[14]

It would appear that in comparative and aggregate
terms the military regime's performance in agriculture
was no worse than that of its civilian predecessor. It
could be argued, however, that in the civilian era the
farmer's sense of importance and his perception of his
status were relatively higher. The announcement of
higher producer prices, in partial response to the high
Udoji awards given to private and public workers, could
help restore some of the desperately sagging morale of
the Nigerian farmer. Producer prices increased from
10 percent to 50 percent.[15]

	Old Price (₦)	New Price (₦)
Cocoa	550	660
Groundnuts	165	250
Palm kernels	132	150
Palm oil	220	280
Soya beans	66	99
Beniseed	176	260
Copra	165	200
Arabic coffee	581	700
Robusta "	506	610
Liberica "	468.50	565

Another measure that could help to repair the farmers'
damaged perception of government's performance was the
reduction of import duties on building materials from
50 percent to a new rate of 20 percent or lower.

As for the mining sector it remained the fastest
growing sector of the Nigerian economy. This could
turn out to be either a curse or a blessing. It could
be a curse for the FMG in that the well-known revenue
from oil had led to extremely high popular expectations for equity. If the FMG failed to satisfy these
expectations political chaos might result. If it could
succeed, so much the better for all. As of 1975 the

people's perception of military performance was mediocre, at best.[16]   The federal government's progress
report and General Gowon's assessments were quite
accurate (see chapters 2 and 5).

All things considered, despite the apparently
lopsided pattern of growth, substantial aggregate
economic progress had been made.   The challenge remained to dovetail promise and plans so as to effect
economic development for all.   Agriculture and manufacturing would have to record more dramatic growth.
Distributive equity could yet be achieved.   That it
was not already secured was not due to callous neglect
but to the factors discussed earlier.   The military
regime's new 1976-80 development plan might accomplish
what the 1970-74 plan did not.

POSTSCRIPT

On the tenth anniversary of the coup d'etat that
brought the Gowon regime to power, the regime found
itself overthrown by members of the same military
organization. Brigadier, now General, Mohammed on
August 1, 1975 gave the many reasons for this overthrow. Among these were "ostentatious living, fla-
grant abuse of office, and deprivation of people's
rights and property." He also contended that the
military governors in the Gowon regime perverted
time-honored government procedures and norms, prac-
ticed nepotism and favoritism, desecrated traditional institutions, and humiliated highly respected
rulers. He asserted that there was "widespread dissatisfaction with former military governors' personal
conduct" and said that they were accused of graft and
misuse of public funds. In a later broadcast on
February 4, 1976 General Mohammed confirmed that ten
of the twelve military governors had been found guilty
of corruption and personal and illegal use of public
funds totaling over ₦16 million.[1]

Assuming that the military who took over reflect
the opinions of most Nigerian military men—and the
many stories and events surrounding the planning and
the execution of the coup d'etat leads one to conclude
that this is the case—a few interpretations relevant
to their performance assessment are possible:

1. They genuinely believed that the Gowon
   regime had not performed well and therefore needed to be replaced, however
   reluctantly.

2. Economic and political development is long-
   range and requires sacrifice, and the interest of the military as well as the nation
   demanded that these be left to the politicians. Such a position does not deny the
   right of the military to come in as a

corporate group when iron surgery is
called for, presumed, or demanded.

3. The Gowon regime, while useful in earlier
years, had outlived its usefulness because
it had failed to demonstrate the kind of
leadership people expect from a military
government.

4. Politicians and Nigerians had registered
sufficiently low performance ratings of
the Gowon regime. In order to extricate
the military from possible chaos a change
of military leadership was imperative.
(There were rumors of junior officers and
ambitious individuals planning to take
over the government).

5. The performance of the regime was so
recognizably low that patriotism called
for its overthrow through the only possible means.

Subsequent actions of the new military regime suggest that it was quite critical of the executive capa-
bility of the civilian bureaucracy—hundreds of bur-
eaucrats including some of the highest placed were dis-
missed or given involuntary and summary retirement.
It had come to accept the fact that economic development need not rule out political participation and
activity and it took steps toward the return of civilian rule. In an editorial comment on this score, the
New Nigerian wrote, "Brigadier Mohammed touched the
heart of the matter when he said that the former regime ignored the true feelings of the people."[2] Finally,
the new regime had become convinced that corruption
and nepotism had not been eradicated as promised, that
they increased under the Gowon regime and that the
country was weary of it—consider the dismissal of the
ten military governors found guilty of corruption.

The overthrow of the Gowon regime and subsequent
events neither invalidated the contentions nor weakened
the overall arguments advanced in this book. Instead
they demonstrate our contention that the subjective
perception of Gowon's regime by the citizenry (particularly relative to economic development) was very low
indeed. The events also show the danger of such low
ratings, objective statistics notwithstanding.

NOTES

Notes: Chapter One

1. See Claude E. Welch, Jr., *Soldier and State in Africa*, particularly the introduction, for a complete catalog of these.

2. Samuel D. Huntington, *Political Order in Changing Society*.

3. This is true of the so-called formal organization school, which will be discussed later in this chapter.

4. Erick A. Nordlinger, "Soldiers in Mufti: The Impact of Military Rule Upon Economic and Social Change in the Non-Western States," *American Political Science Review* 64, no. 4 (December 1970): 1131-48. He concluded that the officer politicians are not interested in fundamental social change and that those soci-etal elements interested in such change will be forced to aban-don their position. Here he has employed extremely limited per-spective and data. To study the social, economic, and political performance of the Nigerian military regime during a raging civil war is unsatisfactory—the major goal at that time was winning the war. Furthermore, the aggregate data used are not relevant given the period they covered. For other studies see Edward Feit, "The Rule of the Iron Surgeon: Military Government in Spain and Ghana," *Comparative Politics* 1, no. 4 (1969): 488-97; Robert Pinkney, *Ghana under Military Rule, 1966-69*; Claude E. Welch, Jr., and Arthur K. Smith, *Military Role and Rule*; James P. Dolian, "The Military and the Allocation of National Resources: An Examination of Thirty-four Sub-Saharan African Nations" (Paper delivered at the International Studies Association Meet-ing, March 14-17, 1973; Samuel Decalo, "The Colonel in the Com-mand Car," *Cultures et Developement,* 4 (1973): 765-78; Henry Bienen, *The Military and Modernization*.

5. Having said this, we must note carefully that where critical assessments of government performance abound both in government and independent press, where the nongovernmental lit-erate elite agree on low performance ratings of the government, and where such low performance ratings transcend the group's particular interests, their probable impact upon the masses can-not be overemphasized.

6. See Dolian, "Military and the Allocation of National Resources."

7. See Irma Adelman and Cynthia Morris, *Society, Politics, and Economic Development: A Quantitative Approach,* especially pp. 13-39.

8. Robert Price, "A Theoretical Approach to Military Rule in New States: Reference Group Theory and the Ghanaian Case," *World Politics* 23, no. 3 (April 1971): 399-430.

9. Ibid, p. 407.

10. *Ghanaian Times,* May 1, 1972, p. 6.

11. In Peter Myer's interview, Colonel Acheampong denied that British influence had made any impact upon him.

12. Huntington, *Political Order,* p. 193.

13. Price, "Theoretical Approach to Military Rule," p. 403.

14. For further discussions of "cross cultural pressures," "role conflict," and "role strain" see Robert Lane, *Political Life,* 1959, and P. J. W. Goode, "A Theory of Role Strain," *American Sociological Review* 25 (1961): 483-96.

15. *Daily Times,* November 20, 1974, p. 1.

16. *Daily Times,* November 22, 1974, pp. 13-14.

17. Morris Janowitz, *The Military in the Political Development of New Nations;* M. J. V. Bell, "The Military in the New States of Africa," in *Armed Forces and Society,* ed. Jacques Van Doorn, pp. 263-64. See also Lyle N. McAlister, *Military and Society in Latin America.*

18. Victor A. Olorunsola, *Societal Reconstruction in Two African States.*

19. Huntington, *Political Order,* pp. 221-22.

20. In this sense the Portuguese military regime is instructive.

Notes: Chapter Two

1. Nigeria, Federal Ministry of Economic Development and

Reconstruction, Central Planning Office, *Second National Development Plan 1970-74, Second Progress Report,* p. 11 (hereafter
cited as *Second Progress Report*).

2. *Daily Times,* October 2, 1974.

3. *Second Progress Report,* p. 33.

4. Ibid., p. 21.

5. Ibid.

6. Ibid., p. 18.

7. Ibid., p. 27.

8. Ibid.

9. Ibid., pp. 48-56. In the Western State about 1,634
acres of rice and 2,096 acres of maize had been cultivated. In
the Mid-Western the "Farmers Crusade" had cultivated 3,700 acres
of rice and 3,000 acres of maize. In the North-Western State
59 group farmers cultivated 550 acres in 1970; 711 group farmers
cultivated 1,781 acres in 1973. In the East-Central State the
Food Production Company produced 16,825 acres of rice, 29,950
acres of maize, and 12,775 acres of cassava. In the East-Central
State 1,636 tons of maize, 770 tons of rice, about five million
tons of yams, and 6,994 bundles of cassava cuttings had been
distributed to farmers. In addition, there were state farm estates. For example, the 6,000 acres of Cowan Oil Palm Estate
belong to the Mid-Western State, and the 16,000 oil palm acres
at Elele belong to the Rivers State. The Rivers State government claimed that input subsidization to 41,648 farmers had been
carried out.

10. Ibid.

11. *Daily Times,* October 2, 1974.

12. *Second Progress Report,* p. 59.

13. Ibid., p. 61.

14. *Daily Times,* October 2, 1974.

15. Ibid.

16. *West Africa,* February 17, 1975, p. 197.

17. *Second Progress Report,* pp. 103-4.

18. *West Africa*, September 16, 1974, p. 1147.

19. Ibid., p. 33.

20. "A major constitutional change was introduced in
October 1972 whereby the Federal Government assumed greater
responsibility in the field. By this change, higher education
which was formerly on the Concurrent Legislative List was transferred to the Exclusive Legislative List while the other levels
of education were transferred to the Concurrent Legislative List.
This change was introduced to enable the Federal Government to
cope more effectively with the task of correcting the imbalances
which were plagueing [*sic*] the nation's educational system. Of
serious concern to the Federal Government was the ever-widening
gap between the northern and southern states of the federation.
A programme which was designed to reduce the gap was approved
by Council for implementation during the 1973-74 financial year.
The programme which was largely tentative pending the formulation of a more detailed programme, was to cost the Federal Government additional ₦13.9 million during the remaining part of
the Plan period. It included the establishment of 12 new Federal Government Colleges for girls, three Advanced Teachers'
Training Colleges in the North-Eastern, Kwara and Benue-Plateau
States, three post-secondary institutions which would offer pre-
university courses, and direct grants to the educationally back-
ward states for the expansion of facilities in their secondary
schools. The Third World Bank loan agreement for ₦36 million
was concluded with the Federal Government on behalf of the six
northern states. This loan was to be utilized to expand and
improve educational facilities at the secondary and teacher
training levels and for expansion of facilities in the School of
Basic Studies in the Faculty of Education at Ahmadu Bello University, Zaria." (*Second Progress Report*, p. 86.)

21. Ibid.

22. General Gowon, in a speech on the occasion of the
opening of the Calabar campus of the University of Nigeria,
Nsukka, said that the 7,700 students of 1966 had expanded to
25,000. He expected enrollment to continue its rapid growth.
(*Africa Research Bulletin* 3287B.)

23. *Daily Times*, October 2, 1974.

24. *Progress Report*, p. 42.

25. Ibid., p. 43.

26. "Though there are unemployment figures, these should

be taken as indicative only. All commentators agree on the inad-
equacy of existing data. If one accepts the data, extrapolating
from the LFSS [Labor Force Sample Survey] at 1 per cent of the
labour force unemployed, using the 1963 census data, by 1971 the
unemployed would be something of the order of 410,000. If one
added the figure of 20 per cent under-employed this would give
5.3 million. From most accounts, the number far from decreasing,
is in fact rising, covering all ages, educational levels and professional skills. The consequences of unemployment--moral, social, political and economic--are too well-known for these to be
worth enumerating. It is sufficient for us to say that no government conscious of its obligations can afford to ignore these.
All governments in the 'developed' states now accept as a goal
and an objective of developing planning some notion of full employment. Only in the developing countries is the reverse the
case. In neither the 1962-68 Plan nor the 1970-74 Plan was employment recognized as a planning objective. In the 1970-74
Plan, though a chapter (34) was given to the employment implications of the plan, it was never an objective per se. The four
year plan simply started out with sectoral investment targets
and then proceeded to work out the employment expected to be
generated. The underlying rationale for ignoring employment was
simply the concern with growth. Growth and employment were seen
as incompatibles and the planners accepted the objective of
growth and only gave secondary recognition to employment. If
Nigeria is to escape serious dysfunctionalities, political and
economic, it would seem that the existing tendency would have to
be reversed. Growth and employment need not be regarded as in-
compatible. In fact, growth could be sacrificed if not enough
attention is given to employment--which has to be recognized as
a primary objective.

"Essentially, for a developing society such as ours, the
problem need not be so acute given that Nigeria now hardly fits
into most models of developing states. We neither fit into a
capital shortage--land surplus, capital shortage--land shortage,
nor a capital surplus--land shortage model. We seem to have a
capital surplus--land surplus model and the problem thus becomes
one of how to maximize employment given that model. In many re-
spects, this resolves into what would be the most desirable
strategies. Negatively, some of the proposals which have been
put forward can hardly be seen as helpful. The argument which
simply relates wage rates to the demand and supply of labour
would seem naively simplistic. Equally, the NYSC device can only
be regarded as a costly but temporary palliative. That conclusion
would also hold for farm settlement schemes.

"Accepting employment as a prime planning objective and
judging from what existing data on unemployment shows, a

multi-dimensional planning strategy would seem to be indicated.
Such a strategy would cover: (a) educational programme directed
at the training of intermediate skilled manpower; non-formal education, e.g. apprenticeships; and retraining of existing manpower. All of this becomes important with the introduction of a
UPE programme; (b) choice of industry and technology oriented at
ensuring mobility of labour and job security." (*Daily Times*,
October 19, 1974, p. 13.)

27. *Second Progress Report*, p. 31.

28. See *Second Progress Report*, p. 32, and General Gowon's
broadcast to the nation, October 1, 1972.

29. *Second Progress Report*, pp. 31-32.

30. Ibid.

31. *Daily Times*, December 28, 1974. pp. 10, 11, 12.

32. *Daily Times*, January 28, 1975.

33. *Daily Times*, January 30, 1975.

34. *Daily Times*, February 8, 1975, p. 7.

35. *Daily Times*, January 29, 1975, p. 1; March 12, 1975.
The Western State government took over the financing, administration, and control of privately owned post-primary schools in the
west as of April 1, 1974 (backdated). To peg down fees and
boarding, grants would be given to proprietors to pay Udoji. The
government retained final say in the opening and closure of
schools, fees payable, and staffing and curriculum. Where proprietors were individuals, mostly honoraria were paid; but community and mission bodies were not eligible.

36. *Daily Times*, January 31, 1975, p. 7.

37. Ibid.

38. Ibid.

39. Ibid.

40. "The Wretched Peoples Union (WPU) is not a political
party. It is neither a cultural organisation, nor is it one of
those parapos that holds a weekly Sunday meeting at the home of
their elders. It is an organisation of the wretched people of
Nigeria who have come together to impress upon the national

government that they too, though they neither belong to the public nor the private sectors of the national economy, are entitled to a decent living as citizens of Nigeria. Because it is not a political organisation, the Wretched Peoples Union holds its meetings in public places.

"I was fortunate to have come across a gathering of these people in an open space in Lagos. On enquiring as to what the fuss was all about, I was pointedly informed that the poor of this country are fast losing their patience. And they were gathered that day to review their situation and decide upon a possible course of action.

"(National Issues) There was not structure to the meeting, yet it was smooth and orderly. I was struck by their awareness and consciousness of national issues. They even know much about Jerome Udoji, his report and the smiles or tears the government White Paper had brought on the faces of a selected Nigerian citizenry.

"'My brothers and sisters,' said the spokesman of the Union, 'we are gathered here today to serve notice to those responsible for our general welfare and happiness that we cannot continue to suffer in silence. We must be heard. We have, like the honorable members of the Nigerian judiciary, suffered neglect that is benign; and deprivation that is unlimited, both in dignified silence. My job this afternoon is to summarise what most of the states' representatives had said.' And so he went on and on, and the list of grievances of the poor of this country seemed endless. The reader of this column no doubt is aware of them.

"However, on this list, a strong emphasis was placed on taxation. He reflected a little on the issue of taxation in this country. The poor people of this country, he said, at the rate they are being taxed would one day be taxed out of existence. Year in and year out, the spokesman emphasised, regardless of whether they earned income or not, they must pay their annual tax. Arbitrary increases of the poor man's tax is a common practice among local authorities in all parts of the country.

"(Negative Tax) After reviewing the problems of the poor and the condition of our rural areas, someone asked: 'What's to be done?' 'I have a plan,' he answered quickly and confidently. 'In the light of the present Udoji exercise, we have come to the inevitable conclusion that there must be negative income tax in this country. I therefore suggest the appointment of our famous Chief Jerome Udoji to head a commission composed of government representatives and those of the chambers of commerce, the working class, journalists and the poor. The commission should

be known as the Nigerian National Commission for the Investigation and Rehabilitation of the Under-privileged. His term of
reference should be to study the problem of urban and rural
poverty with a view to harmonising the two. Just as Chief Udoji
was able to suggest a minimum wage scale for workers in the public sector, he should come up with the least amount of income to
be earned by the average Nigerian to escape the affliction of
poverty. This income level should be known as the Nigerian
National Poverty Line (NNPL). In view of the current economic
situation, we have come to the conclusion that every Nigerian
family head earning an income of less than ₦600 per annum should
be designated as poor. Not only should his income go untaxed,
but the government should feel duty bound to make up for the difference between his earned income and the Nigerian National Poverty Line. This, therefore, explains my principle of negative
income tax.'

"'But don't you think you are asking too much from the government?' asked one of the delegates from the South Eastern
states.

"'My friend,' retorted the spokesman of the wretched poor,
'ask not what your country cannot afford to give you but you can
ask for what you can conveniently get from your country. We did
not ask for this equitable distribution of the national wealth
when this country was living off groundnuts, cocoa and palm oil.
We are asking for it now because Nigeria is wealthy enough to
lend money to the World Bank and according to Dr. Isong, governor
of the Central Bank, we have billions of naira sitting in his
safe gathering dust.'

"When I left that meeting, I had an eerie feeling that the
case of the poor in Nigeria is a genuine one. Although they have
remained non-vocal for long, history has shown that an army of
poor people or their advocates have changed the course of history, often for the better." (*Daily Times*, February 9, 1975,
p. 9.)

41. *Daily Times*, October 2, 1972, p. 1.

42. *Daily Times*, February 8, 1973, p. 28.

43. *Daily Times*, September 5, 1973, p. 3. The public servants said that the rent subsidy would negate principles of justice and fair play. According to the *Daily Times*: The Nigerian
Civil Service Union "alleged that in the past five years, some
top civil servants had awarded all available benefits to only
the administrative class, to the utter neglect of other classes
of workers. . . . According to the union, the new rent circular

had caused widespread depression, demoralisation and annoyance among civil servants outside the administrative class in all the states of the country." The *Sunday Times*, (September 2, 1973, p. 13) reported that Scale C officers had protested to the Head of S ate concerning "the practice of 'class distinction' in an indigenous civil service whereby categories of officers are placed in very advantageous positions and are consequently getting the best of everything including salaries, allowances and fringe benefits in a most annoying and provocative manner." While those on Scale C living outside government quarters pay "prohibitive rents ranging from ₦600 to ₦1,200 per annum in unfurnished flats, those on Scale 'A' and higher graded officers who had been enjoying maximum comfort in government quarters at normal rents have been given further and indefensible rent relief."

44. *Daily Times*, October 6, 1973.

45. *Daily Times*, November 26, 1973, p. 2.

46. *Daily Times*, December 15, 1974, p. 7.

47. *West Africa*, September 16, 1974, p. 1146.

48. *Daily Times*, December 15, 1974, p. 7.

49. Ibid., pp. 7, 11.

Notes: Chapter Three

1. *Daily Times*, November 12, 1973, p. 7.

2. *Daily Times*, February 27, 1975, p. 7.

3. See Hon. Awolowo, *Anglo-Nigerian Military Pact Agreement, Press Conference*, November 23, 1960 (Nigeria: Action Group Bureau of Information, 1960) for the issues involved.

4. See Lewis Coser, *The Functions of Social Conflict*.

5. In this case the educated African portrayed by Chinua Achebe in many of his novels may be misleading, except if viewed in the context of traditional societal values.

6. "An Address by the Visitor, His Excellency Major General Yakubu Gowon at the 21st Foundation Day Ceremony of the University of Ibadan," November 17, 1969.

7. Gowon's remarks to university students, *New Nigeria*, October 5, 1971, p. 10.

8. France, Tanzania, the Ivory Coast, and the United States were variously their targets.

9. On January 24, 1974 the public relations officer for NUNS, Tunde Thompson, said that military rulers should "hasten to hand over [government] to civilians by 1976." He called for the setting up of a constituent assembly "without delay" to determine the type of constitution for the country. He wanted students to be represented and warned African leaders against an arrogance of power and designs to stay in office perpetually. "All those who are now busy discrediting the politicians should remember that not all of them were bad during the First Republic of Nigeria. . . . There is no need to be pessimistic about the restoration of full political activity." (*Africa Research Bulletin*, section C, January 1-31, 1974, p. 3121.)

10. *Daily Times*, May 28, 1969, pp. 1, 3.

11. See Olorunsola, *Societal Reconstruction*, chap. 7, 11.

12. On the first two points see *West Africa*, February 7, 1971, p. 178, and February 19, 1971, p. 205. Regarding the third point, thousands of market women joined the student demonstrations in 1971 (see later discussions in this chapter).

13. In their public remarks most military leaders preferred to see them as political tools manipulated by civilians with political ambition.

14. *West Africa*, April 9, 1973, p. 482, and October 16, 1972, p. 1404.

15. *Christian Science Monitor*, July 13, 1973.

16. Yakubu Gowon, Convocation Address, Ahmadu Bello University, December 2, 1972.

17. *West Africa*, February 23, 1973.

18. *West Africa*, April 9, 1973, p. 482.

19. *West Africa*, April 2, 1973, p. 441.

20. *West Africa*, April 30, 1973, p. 581.

21. *West Africa*, February 24, 1975.

22. "Four years ago, when I gave 1976 as the target date for returning the country to normal constitutional government, both myself and the military hierarchy honestly believed that by that date, especially after a bloody civil war for which there had been a great deal of human and material sacrifice and from which we had expected that every Nigerian would have learnt a lesson, there would have developed an atmosphere of sufficient stability. We had thought that genuine demonstration of moderation and self-control in pursuing sectional ends in the overall interest of the country would have become the second nature of all Nigerians.

"Regrettably, from all the information at our disposal, from the general attitude, utterances and manoeuvres of some individuals and groups and from some publications during the past few months, it is clear that those who aspire to lead the nation on the return to civilian rule have not learnt any lesson from our past experiences. In spite of the existence of a state of emergency which has so far precluded political activity, there have already emerged such a high degree of sectional politicking, intemperate utterances and writings which were deliberately designed to whip up ill-feelings within the country to the benefit of the political aspirations of a few. There is no doubt that it would not take them long to return to the old cut-throat politics that once led this nation into serious crises. We are convinced that this is not what the honest people of this country want. What the country and the ordinary citizen want is peace and stability, the only condition under which progress and development are possible.

"Our own assessment of the situation as of now is that it will be utterly irresponsible to leave the nation in the lurch by a precipitate withdrawal which will certainly throw the nation back into confusion. Therefore, the Supreme Military Council, after careful deliberation and full consultation with the hierarchy of the Armed Forces and Police, have decided that the target date of 1976 is in the circumstance unrealistic and that it would indeed amount to a betrayal of trust to adhere rigidly to that target date. I want to make it abundantly clear, however, that we have not abandoned the idea of returning to civilian rule. We consider it our responsibility to lay the foundation of a self-sustaining political system which can stand the test of time in such a manner that each national political crisis does not become a threat to the nation's continued existence as a single entity and which will ensure a smooth and orderly transition from one government to another. To this end, the Federal Military Government will appoint, in due course, a panel to draw up a new draft constitution which when approved by the Government will be referred to the people for adoption in a manner to be

determined. Meanwhile, the ban on partisan political activities
still remains in force. The Federal Military Government proposed
to broaden the scope of participation in government by the people.
Accordingly, councils comprising persons drawn from a cross section of the country will be established both at federal and state
levels to advise the government." (*Daily Times*, October 2, 1974,
p. 1.)

23. At the University of Ife, the students called on Tarka
to resign, saying that otherwise Nigeria would be viewed as "a
nation without a conscience." They called Tarka's attitude "dis-
gusting and unpatriotic." To them it "revealed utmost contempt
for public opinion and an intolerable disdain for the best tradition of public service." (Quoted in the *Daily Times*, July 28,
1974, p. 1.) At the University of Benin the students called for
the promulgation of an anticorruption decree, saying, "As a corrective regime the military should not just pick up a few top
officers as 'scape goats' but embark on a total clean up of the
society" (*Daily Times*, August 2, 1974, p. 1). Two Yoruba briga-
diers had been compelled to retire for associating with "questionable persons." The students of the University of Lagos expressed similar sentiments. Ultimately the commissioner resigned.

24. *Daily Times*, September 8, 1974, p. 1.

25. Ibid.

26. "No political organisations. No mass meetings. No
public demonstrations. No parliament. The country is still
under a state of emergency. The Press is threatened. The Judiciary is warned. What next? The threat of the Inspector-General
of Police to the Press, a fortnight ago, was not unusual. In
many countries, at any time when the Press is engaged in a crusade that embarrasses any government it is not uncommon for
highly placed men in the government to warn the Press that it
was going beyond its bounds. Former American Vice-President
Spiro Agnew threatened the US Press. British Prime Minister
Harold Wilson had harsh things to say about the UK Press. You
can multiply that in many countries where the government is
elected, selected, or imposed. The Press of Nigeria is, therefore, used to threats from governments--colonial, civilian and
armed forces.

"But is the Judiciary also used to warnings? In July, a
citizen felt so strongly about what he honestly believed to be
the corrupt practices of a member of the Federal Government. He
wrote letters stating the facts to the heads of the army, police,
navy, cabinet office etc. No action was taken on his letter,
much less to acknowledge receipt. In a mood of righteous

indignation he went to court to swear an affidavit to assure the authorities that he knew what he was talking about and would accept any punishment that the law may impose for making false statements on oath. As a result of his disclosures, the police investigated his allegations and the two Ps (Police and Press) findings and pressures forced the Commissioner of Communications Joseph Tarka, to resign from office. Note that the Judicial Advisory Committee did not breathe a word throughout the historic drama.

"In August, another citizen swore to an affidavit alleging corruption against Benue Plateau State Governor, Joseph Gomwalk. Again, the Press investigated and publicised the allegations. It was presumed that the police were also conducting their own investigation; at least until last Saturday when the Head of State announced that Governor Gomwalk was not guilty of any act of corruption. The Judicial Advisory Committee did not breathe a word when Aku filed his affidavit against Governor Gomwalk, when he was detailed by the police and when his wife filed a writ of *habeas corpus* for his release. But 48 hours after the Head of State had absolved Governor Gomwalk of any guilt and warned judges not to allow themselves to be used for embarrassing government functionaries, the Judicial Advisory Committee issued a statement declaring that the courts would no longer accept affidavits alleging corruption and improprieties against any person.

"The question which all right-thinking persons would ask is: Where was the Judicial Advisory Committee throughout the Tarka-Daboah imbroglio? Three weeks after Tarka resigned, the judges and chief justices met in Lagos but made no pronouncement on the use of affidavits to expose Tarka. The Aku affidavit was sworn to and published in the newspaper last week. The Judicial Advisory Committee did not feel sufficiently concerned that a process of law was misused. The learned members of the Judicial Advisory Committee appeared to have waited until the Head of State who appointed them spoke on the issue before they hurriedly met and issued a statement. When the Press is threatened and the Judiciary warned, it is darkness visible." (*Daily Times*, September 11, 1974, p. 1.)

27. *Daily Times*, August 28, 1974, p. 3, contains the press release on this subject.

28. *Daily Times*, September 18, 1974, p. 1.

29. "The students of the Ahmadu Bello University, Zaria, have joined in the demand for the immediate release of a Gboko businessman, Mr. Aper Aku, now being held in detention. Making

a passionate appeal to the Federal Government to effect the in-
stant release of Mr. Aku, the president of the university students' union, Malam Adamu Maina Waziri, said the continued detention of Mr. Aku was widening the credibility gap of the military
regime. Malam Waziri, who was speaking at the opening of the
1974/75 students' parliament, declared that if the point-by-point
falsification of the claim of Mr. Aku in his affidavit by Governor Joseph Gomwalk was not enough, the detainee should be taken
to court for prosectuion without further delay.

"Calling on the Federal Government to approach the detention of Nigerians with rationality, the students said affidavits
against corruption should immediately be legalised to eradicate
the ills which they contended had become a national catastrophe.
On the Nigerian Press, Malam Waziri condemned the frequent arrest
and detention of journalists and columnists adding that such acts
'assassinate' the purported freedom of Nigerians." (*Daily Times*,
November 25, 1974, p. 1.)

30. James C. Scott, *Comparative Political Corruption*
(Englewood Cliffs, N.J.: Prentice Hall, 1972), p. 3.

31. "Students of our universities whose action led to the
closure of three universities were clearly wrong in the intemperate abusive languages of their placards and their violent destruction of property. The *Daily Times* acknowledges the right of any
group of people to have their say, to carry placards and to stage
peaceful demonstrations, to talk sense and nonsense within the
bounds of reason and limitations of the law. But violence?
'babu', 'mba', 'ra-ra', 'no'. We strongly condemn the vandalism
of the students in setting fire to property and equipment. There
can be no justification whatsoever for such utterly irresponsible
action. It was a selfish and self-destructive action; for what
do they want to use when all these are over and what do they want
those coming behind them to use after so much destruction?

"Of course, the *Daily Times* shares the thinking of the students that a programme of gradual and peaceful return to democratic rule should be reopened. We share their view that the
continued detention of citizens without trial is wrong. A review
of the war-time emergency regulations is also long overdue. But
all right-thinking Nigerians should realise that the transfer of
political power from the Armed Forces to democratically-elected
representatives of the people unless it is negotiated and the
programme mutually agreed with the Armed Forces, could lead to
anarchy. Those who were old enough to witness the lawlessness in
Western Nigeria in 1965 and the direct and indirect impacts of
the civil war that followed, would not want a repetition of such
anarchy as a means of achieving political ideals, however lofty."

(*Daily Times*, February 19, 1975, p. 3.)

    32. Ibid.

    33. *Daily Times*, February 15, 1975, p. 7.

    34. *Daily Times*, February 27, 1975, p. 7.

    35. *Daily Times*, February 23, 1975, p. 28; February 27, 1975, p. 1.

    36. *Daily Times*, March 1, 1975, pp. 1, 3.

    37. "The Federal and Western State governments' order that Universities of Ife, Ibadan and Lagos should remain closed until further notice, thus nullifying the decision of the Senates of these institutions is ill-advised. In addition to rendering the Senates impotent, the order also amounts to interference in the affairs of these universities. The actions of the two governments also raise the crucial issues of the autonomy of our universities, the appointment of vice-chancellors and the powers of Visitors.

    "As far as we know, the Vice-Chancellors, acting on the advice of their Senates are the most competent authorities to decide the most congenial time to reopen universities shut down as a result of student disturbances. Neither the Universities' Councils nor their Visitors are constitutionally empowered to interfere with such matters. Besides, it was the Senates and not the Visitors which rusticated the students and shut down the institutions. And in taking that prompt and therefore highly commendable action, the Senates were acting within their powers. It is therefore only logical that the authorities that ordered the closure of the universities should be allowed to decide when to reopen them.

    "But by overruling the decisions of the Senates, the Federal and Western State governments have destroyed the authorities of the supreme academic bodies of these institutions, a situation that negates their autonomy and academic freedom. But if, as it were, the two governments were playing the part of piper dictating the tune, then their actions must be seen as justifying our view that the continued appointment of vice-chancellors by government unquestionably detracts from the autonomy of these institutions. The Udoji Commission had foreseen this kind of conflict when it recommended that the Senate be entrusted with the appointment of vice-chancellors. But the Federal Government in its White Paper on the Report had turned it down, on the excuse, which we consider not altogether defensible, that past experience

had shown that tribal acrimony over a similar appointment made
Udoji's recommendation undesirable.

"Yet it is essential that our universities, like their
counterparts elsewhere in the world, should not only be autono-
mous but seen to be so in practice. It is therefore our view
borne out of experience that the world-wide practice of the
appointment of vice-chancellors by the Senate be applicable to
Nigeria. Meanwhile, it is in the interest of all concerned that
nothing should be done to expose the Senates to ridicule. For
it will be a sad day for both the universities and the nation
when the Senates lose their traditional respect and control over
these institutions." (*Daily Times*, February 28, 1975, p. 3.)

38. "On Wednesday, February 26, the Federal Government
issued a public statement to the effect that 'it would be premature' to reopen the three universities [Ife, Lagos and Ibadan]
which, some two weeks earlier, had been closed to students by
internal decisions of the respective university authorities.
The reason advanced by government for the counter-measure of continued closure was 'because the situation which was precipitated
by the student unrest . . . has not returned to normal.' Presumably, the ultimate justification of government's negatively
protective action derived from fears of threat to national security and thus to peace, order and good government within the universities themselves. Any well-meaning citizen will of course
recognise that the government is in a vantage (though not necessarily the best or monopoly) position to pronounce on possible
threats to security; that it has a right--indeed an obligatory
duty--to take anticipatory measures against such latent or incipient threats; and that it need not disclose to the public the
nature or extent of these or assumed security threats. For a
military government, the easy and prompt exercise of strong and
arbitrary powers is not only tempting but understandable, even
when the threat-to-security argument is now widely appreciated
by the lay public. But any impartial observer watching the drama
of government and universities relation over the last two years,
and particularly, over the last two weeks, cannot but conclude
that the government's statement of February 26 is another nail in
the coffin of mutual trust and respect between the two. The se-
quence of events is clearly such that if government had wanted,
the resulting conflict of moral and administrative authority that
is now exhibited to both the student population and the general
public would have been avoided. As it happened, the government
apparently chose a procedure which did not take the university
into its confidence about its threat-to-security fears before
the latter's decision to announce their reopening decisions.
Unless, of course, the Vice-Chancellors had some vital information all along or at some critical points along the way but which
they did not pass on to their academic colleagues!

"We could not but ponder at some procedural issues. Were the governmental authorities (especially the Visitors) formally or informally aware of the intention of the university authorities to consider reopening of their institutions to students? Were the respective Senates warned through gentle hint or harsh notice to the Vice-Chancellors that it might not be wise to contemplate such thoughts before the Senates made their recommendation? Did the Committee of Vice-Chancellors during their meeting in Lagos around February 21 seize the opportunity to learn any possible security grounds against their recommendation of reopening? Was there not enough time between the inexplicable (but nevertheless effected) publication of the Committee of Vice-Chancellors' recommendation and the deliberations by respective Senates three or four days later for the government to hint the substance of its countermanding announcement that came six days after the published basic recommendation of the committee? Perhaps, for the moment, answers to these questions are neither necessary nor important. The fact of the moment is that the three universities remain closed to students for an indefinite period, and for reasons which are beyond the control and against the recommendation of the university authorities. What are the implications of this fact and what are likely to be its probable consequences?

"In its announcement, the government itself seemed to appreciate that final year students would be adversely affected by prolonged closure and that this is a 'critical period in the university calendar.' What it probably failed to appreciate is that under the course system of degree programmes, virtually the entire student body would indeed suffer considerable hardships of undigested crowded lecture materials, uncompleted practicals and tutorial assignments, unsatisfied prerequisite requirements, inadequate exposure to and guidance by staff, low examination performance in the stiff face of avoiding lower test standards and general emotional upset arising from inevitable disruptions to normal academic calendar and work flow. When these problems are related to special students like those in clinical or postgraduate programmes, the real personal and social costs are incalculable. Some may have to repeat a whole session, as a direct or indirect consequence of prolonged closure under conditions of uncertainty. The academic session cannot be indefinitely extended without affecting the 1975-76 programme and students' intake. It is a disconcerting thought that the present stalemate may involve the nation in sacrificing one full generation of graduates. What affects the students affects their parents, guardians, teachers, government and the nation at large.

"We do not want to be misinterpreted to be supporting irresponsible action or wanton destruction by students, or indeed by any social group. We have, in fact jointly and severally

condemned the misguided action of the few who sometimes overdra-
matise their protests. But we must reiterate on this occasion,
the substance and essential ingredients of the students' social
demands appear legitimate. We believe we can embrace their
ideals while condemning their methods. To the extent that academic considerations should enter into public policy decision-
making, we also believe that the universities are in the best
position to exercise judgment and offer advice. On academic
grounds, we are convinced that the nation would lose more by continued closure of the universities than it would gain in the long
run from a posture of apparently knocking fear, if not sense,
into the students through uncertainty and indefinite closure.
The tragedy of the present position is that by slapping the university authorities in the face publicly the government is (perhaps unwittingly) creating the further impression of wanting to
humiliate the academics as the occasion demands and make them
lose moral authority both with the public and before their own
students. All we can say here is that this is a game which the
government can win some of the time and for quite some time. But
experience has shown that in the universal struggle for intellec-
tual dignity, university autonomy, democratic freedom and pro-
gressive social policies, the mere monopoly of arbitrary powers
and legalised physical violence is no substitute for reason,
integrity and consistency of selfless principles." (*Daily Times*,
March 6, 1975, pp. 14, 15.)

39. *Daily Times*, March 7, 1975, p. 5.

40. "The communique was signed by the national president of
NUNS, Mr. Henry Ejembi, and the national vice-president, Mr.
Austin Ukori, as well as 24 others representing all universities
and higher institutions of learning in the country" (*Daily Times*,
March 5, 1975, p. 3).

41. *Daily Times*, February 10, 1975, p. 1.

42. "The attention of the National Association of Resident
Doctors has been drawn to the Press statement by the Federal Commissioner for Information, Mr. Edwin Clark, on the detention of
five Nigerians under the provisions of the emergency powers.
These men were accused of being involved in various acts inimical
to the interests of the Federal Government. He also stated,
inter alia: 'During the doctor's strike the group maintained con-
stant contact with junior doctors and helped to publicise their
case.' The National Association of Resident Doctors hereby
states categorically and emphatically that there is no iota of
truth in the assertion of this newly appointed federal commissioner for information of collusion between resident doctors and
any of these men. The NARD has never required the assistance of

any individual or groups in publicising its aims, intentions or
demands. We will like to recall that as far back as December 3,
1974, our views were made known in clear terms through our memo-
randum which was submitted to the head of the Federal Government.
We wish to inform this new federal commissioner for information
that while he was still in the Mid-West, it was clear to the Federal Government that it was the Nigerian Medical Association (and
not the junior doctors) that was actively looking after the interest of all Nigerian doctors during the doctors industrial action.   It is also our contention that the Federal Government
was, in no doubt, as to the sincerity of our purpose and the integrity of our members. It is pertinent to point out at this
stage that the Nigerian Medical Association is presently engaged
in negotiations with the Federal Government to find a lasting
solution to the problem that led to the last dispute. Therefore,
any such reckless and unjustified outburst from high quarters is
most unhelpful and counter-productive.

"This wild claim of the federal commissioner for information is an unwarranted insult to the rank and file Nigerian doctors. While we appreciate this honorable commissioner's enthusiasm to justify his appointment, the Nigerian doctors will not
succumb to any attempt by anyone to make them a 'sacrificial
lamb.' We, therefore, challenge the federal commissioner for
information to substantiate this wild claim of his or, in the
alternative, he should have the courtesy to withdraw his claim.
The NARD seizes this opportunity to appeal to all Nigerians to
exercise utmost restraint in their public utterances." (*Daily
Times*, March 6, 1975, p. 28.)

43. "We have tried to correct this impression, but it appears the government is determined to make a scapegoat of us,
since it is not ready to listen to our plea of innocence. We
want to make it clear that we have no connection whatsoever with
any person or persons, who, according to a recent government
statement, are involved in activities calculated to discredit
the Federal Government. . . . We need nobody to teach us that
detention without trial or reason is not good. At our age, and
level of education, we do not need any special lecture on the
advantages of free education at all levels and free medical services. These we have called for with the best of intentions and
for the good of the government and the country. Like students
all over the world, we owe our nation a duty to justify her investment in our education by being alive to happenings around us.
We do not oppose the detention of any group that would want to
indulge in mischievous activities to the detriment of peace and
stability in our country. But it is our opinion that such people
could still be efficiently dealt with without emergency decree
24." (*Daily Times*, March 8, 1975, p.1, and March 12, 1975, p.3.)

44. *Daily Times*, March 12, 1975, p. 7.

45. Ibid.

46. For methodology and details of findings see Olorunsola, *Societal Reconstruction*, chap. 11.

47. Ibid.

48. Ibid., chaps. 7, 11.

49. *Daily Times*, March 13, 1975, p. 1.

50. *Daily Times*, March 14, 1975, p. 11.

51. *Daily Times*, March 12, 1975, p. 7.

52. *Daily Times*, March 8, 1975, p. 28.

53. *Daily Times*, March 12, 1975, p. 7.

54. "The warning is contained in a statement issued in Ibadan yesterday by police public relations officer Superintendent Emmanuel Gbiwon on behalf of the state police commissioner, Alhaji Kafaru Tinubu. He said: 'The public is hereby warned that the police will not tolerate this irresponsible action and will deal very severely with anyone found to be connected with the setting up of these illegal road blocks.' He assured those farmers wishing to take their goods to the market for sale that the police would protect their lives and property.

"Investigation carried out in Ibadan and its environs revealed that since the past two weeks, there had been considerable increase in the prices of foodstuff like yams, cassava flour, beans, rice, gari, onion bulbs, palm oil, fruits and vegetables, as a result of some farmers' action. The farmers, according to sources, refused to sell to traders their farm products. Among their alleged demands were the reduction in the prices of building materials and transport fare which, according to the sources, had risen astronomically a few months ago. The farmers allegedly claimed that as a result of the high cost of living and building materials, many of them found it extremely difficult to erect a house or plaster their houses with cement. The farmers, I gathered, are also demanding reduction in the prices of insecticides and fertilizers. They are, in addition, demanding a substantial increase in prices of cash crops to alleviate their financial hardship as a result of the present high cost of living in the country." (*Daily Times*, March 14, 1975, p. 3.)

55. *Daily Times*, March 21, 1975, p. 1.

56. *Daily Times*, October 27, 1973, p. 6.

57. *Daily Times*, March 24, 1975, p. 4.

58: Olorunsola, *Societal Reconstruction*, chap. 11.

59. *Daily Times*, January 31, 1975, p. 16.

60. " Interviews conducted at Oritamerin, Gege and other big food distribution centres in the Western State capital yesterday showed that gari, rice, yam and beans were in short supply. Because of the high demand for the little quantity available for sale, selling prices have risen to more than double their prices a year ago. The current price index shows that prices have gone up by 70 to 300 per cent. Among other factors given for the shortage is the increase in the cost of transportation of goods from distant areas to the big cities. Also, the farmers complained that the cost of cultivation had gone up as laborers demanded their own Udoji." (*Daily Times*, March 21, 1975, p. 1.)

61. "The housewives see all their suffering and hardship as the hard-work of the 'selfish' and 'greedy' market women who have taken advantage of the Udoji awards to arbitrarily inflate prices to the point of making it impossible for some people to eat one decent meal a day.

"The wife of a night guard, a woman whose husband earns less than ₦42 a month, lamented that her family of five might die of slow starvation unless something is done to improve the situation. She complained that formerly 50 kobo was enough for her to cook a pot of soup which lasted the family for at least two days. Now ₦1.50 kobo is hardly enough to prepare the same pot of soup.

"The wife of someone who earns what could be called a decent salary (something in the neighborhood of ₦4000 per annum) says she needs at least ₦5.00 for a decent pot of soup which the family finishes the same day. These two women are typical examples of the numerous housewives who blame their plight on the 'get-rich-quick' attitude of the market women whose main business they claim is to suck them dry since they have heard about the Udoji bonanza. The housewives also claimed that the scarcity of housemaids which has been with us for some time now has been further accentuated by the Udoji awards. 'The girls are making impossible demands and a housewife either accepts their terms or loses them to more "generous" employers. They now want to be

treated like demi-gods.' Both factions--the housemaids and market women--however have their own side of the story to tell."
(*Daily Times,* January 31, p. 16.)

62. Ibid.

63. Ibid.

64. Ibid.

65. Olorunsola, *Societal Reconstruction.*

Notes: Chapter Four

1. *New Nigerian,* October 1, 1971.

2. *West Africa,* March 29, 1969, p. 1197.

3. *West Africa,* December 17, 1971, p. 1471.

4. *West Africa,* March 17, 1972, p. 337.

5. *Daily Times,* March 3, 1975, p. 7.

6. *Daily Times,* February 23, 1975, p. 7.

7. Ibid., p. 3.

8. "Nigerians need not be reminded that this is a military
regime. The absence of an elected parliament and political parties, and the all too frequent rowdy behavior of soldiers on the
street and other public places are enough to keep people informed
that ours is not a civilian regime. However, this situation does
not alter the basic fact that the government--whether civilian or
military--has some obligations to the governed. This includes
the right of the governed to express their views on the performance of those governing them and the right to ask when basic
promises made to them are to be fulfilled.

"It was, therefore, gratuitous of the governor of Lagos
State to remind viewers of WNTV [Western Nigeria Television] last
Thursday that the governors had not been elected by the masses
who presumably therefore have no right to ask when they are to be
changed. This statement shows a singular lack of political sen-
sitivity and lack of awareness (or is it indifference?) of public
interest in the subject. One of the major causes of the difficulties facing our governments today is the communication gap
between the government and the governed. Forums such as the one

offered by the WNTV should therefore be used properly by those in government to enlighten the public on various aspects of the country's affairs. It should never be used by any government functionary to inflame tempers or mislead the public." (*New Nigerian*, March 24, 1975, p. 1.)

9. *Daily Times*, March 29, 1975, p. 2.

10. *New Nigerian*, September 17, 1974, p. 1.

11. *New Nigerian*, October 16, 1974, p. 1.

12. *Daily Times*, September 21, 1974, p. 3.

13. *Daily Times*, November 5, 1974, p. 3.

14. "Lately, the problem of increased food production to feed Nigeria's rapidly growing population has generated a lot of public debate. Several suggestions have been made by well-placed Nigerians about how to raise agricultural out put and modernise farming. The suggestion by Mr. M. A. Eyo, South-Eastern State Commissioner for Agriculture and Natural Resources, has brought a new dimension to this all important debate. Mr. Eyo has suggested that unless a corps of educated people and professional agriculturists in Nigeria become farmers, the future of agriculture is bleak. This is no prophecy of doom. Something radical and decisive must be done to revolutionise agriculture in Nigeria within the shortest time possible. To this end, the prospects of trained agriculturists setting up their own model farms in their own locality look like a more attractive alternative to the over-capitalised and less productive farm settlements. But to set up his own model farm, the agriculturist needs some capital and the various governments should be prepared to help him financially to his feet. Of course, any loans made to him will be repayable after some time. This is a better arrangement than having agricultural officers waste away in extension services that have so far not justified the huge sums of money sunk in them. An agricultural officer who sets up a model farm in his locality has the advantage of ready acceptability by the local farmers and problems of communication will not arise at all.

"The clarion call for young people to go back to the farm should be examined against the urgent need to introduce modern and cheap farming tools. Farming at present holds no attraction for the school leaver if he has to use the old tools used by his great-grandfather. One of the tasks of agricultural research is to devise new implements to replace the antiquated ones now being used by most of our farmers. Attention should also be focused on problems of soil conservation. There is also the need for

governments, through local authorities, to work out an arrangement that will ensure security of tenure for a land holder over
a reasonable time.

"As suggested by the Agricultural Society of Nigeria, emphasis should be placed on farmers' education to get people more
involved in food and cash crop production. Happily, some states
have started the teaching of agriculture in primary and secondary
schools. Other states should follow this example so that the
message of the agricultural revolution can reach every corner of
the federation." (*Daily Times*, July 17, 1974, p. 3.)

15. "Undoubtedly, the ₦14,000 bonus, which is said to be
earmarked for deserving farmers by the Rivers State Government,
in appreciation of the farmers' response to the state's increased
food production campaign last year, will serve as an incentive
and motivation, not only to the receiving farmers, but to farmers
in general. This new idea of giving rewards for hard work should
be emulated by other states because it is important that the
farmers should produce enough for local consumption as well as
for export. But the reward should not be limited to monetary
awards only. The farmers should be given an adequate storage
system. At present, our farmers are at the mercy of the middle-
man to whom they sell food crops at give-away prices in order not
to suffer great losses through unsold farm products that may be
spoilt during the harvesting season. Undoubtedly the exploitation by the middlemen greatly hinders the farmers' chance of making any appreciable profit. If the state governments, under the
guidance of the Ministries of Agriculture, can provide storage
systems for the farmers' food crops, the sale of these products
can be spread throughout the years, thereby reducing the present
price fluctuations from which farmers suffer. The state's Ministries of Agriculture can also examine the possibility of renting
out, on a larger scale than at present, heavy machineries to the
local farmer. With this, considerable modernisation of their
methods would be achieved. It may not be enough to give the
farmers innovative ideas without the necessary tools to implement
them.

"And the rural women, who form an appreciable percentage of
the rural community, should not be left out in the efforts to
encourage the rural population. They should be brought in at all
levels of reorganisation since they handle the selling, and whatever preservation there is, of farm products. It is thus necessary that the rural women should be considered as an integral
section of the people who must be motivated. To keep ignoring
them would be a grave over-sight.

"Besides, the new incentives to farmers and efforts to help

in the modernisation of their activities can be partly channelled
through the co-operative movements, which happily enough, are
now being encouraged by the various state governments. The present emphasis and interest in the farmers must continue in order
to ensure steady expansion in agricultural output and harmonise
relations between the urban and rural population." (*Daily Times*,
April 4, 1974, p. 3.)

     16. "One of the government-owned companies that has often
come under severe public criticism is the marketing board. This
is because the decisions and activities of the marketing boards
affect about 70 per cent of Nigeria's working population, who
are engaged in farming. And for the country as a whole, the welfare of the farmers is to a large extent the welfare of every
Nigerian. For it is only when the farmers are given adequate
price and other incentives that they could be encouraged to produce more to feed and provide more foreign exchange earnings for
the nation.

     "Yet, the operation of the marketing board system has in
recent years not been able to satisfy the demands of farmers.
Their major grievance is that the prices they receive from the
marketing boards for their products are by far lower than the
world market prices for the exportable commodities. In short,
although our farmers are known to be hard-working, their returns
are low. The buying agents of the marketing boards also help to
worsen the plight of the farmers. They under-weigh the produce
of the farmers with the result that the latter's returns are further reduced. In many cases, they do not pay the farmers immediately after their produce have been collected by the agents.
This lack of immediate cash payment further makes life difficult
for the farmers.

     "A reform plan for the produce marketing system was an-
nounced during this year's budget. Among the reform measures
was the abolition of existing duty and produce taxes on agricultural commodities and the substitution of a 10 per cent produce
tax. Moreover, price fixing was to become the responsibility of
a central machinery, presumably the Nigerian Produce Marketing
Company. Our view of the reform is that the farmers may not be
very much better off than before. The produce tax is still high,
in the sense that it will take much of what should be the farmers'
legitimate returns. Even assuming that the reform will help the
farmers, there is no indication so far that it has been implemented. Although this is a general weakness in our planning procedure, the problems of the agricultural sector are such that any
reform contemplated should be implemented with utmost urgency.
The reform should also take into account the scrutiny of the
types of licensed buying agents appointed to deal directly with

the farmers. We call on the Federal Government not only to re-
examine the plight of the farmers, but also to speed up action
on the reform of the marketing board system." (*Daily Times*,
August 9, 1973, p. 3.)

17. *New Nigerian*, August 1, 1974, p. 1.

18. *Daily Times*, August 12, 1974, p. 1.

19. "All the talks about damaged jetty or unavailable parts
should be a thing of the past since we expect that experience
should have by now taught us how to get the best out of the
plant. As it is quite clear that it should take some time before
we can refine enough oil for our own use, arrangements should be
made for steady importation of our supplementary need. Mr. Asiodu
has not yet given an indication as to where the extra three of
four refineries shall be located. We hope that when the sites
are to be eventually decided, they would be chosen with an eye to
maximum efficiency and convenience of the ordinary citizen. In
any case, we advocate that plans should be made right away to
combat whatever pollution must necessarily arise from the instal-
lation of these refineries.

"To round up, we suggest that more of our oil money should
be diverted to mechanised and co-operative farming; that more
efficient arrangements should be made to ensure that petroleum
products are available in sufficient quantities to keep the
nation's economic activities flowing smoothly; that the proposed
additional refineries be located to the optimum advantage of the
whole nation; and that steps be taken to ensure that foreign oil
companies in the country make positive contribution to the
nation's progress in all possible ways. Nigeria is said to be
number nine in the league of world oil producers. We must not
allow a minority to swim in petroleum affluence while the majority suffer in the midst of plenty." (*Daily Sketch*, July 30,
1974, p. 1.)

20. "As for the wisdom of utilisation of existing oil revenue, the issue is an open debate. Quite obviously, there have
been many reports of contracts signed, financial commitment on
various projects, but it is still to be seen how the quality of
life of common man has improved despite the oil boom. Or is the
oil boom too boomy for efficient management by our economic planners? The fear of oil being a wasting asset, of imported inflation swallowing foreign exchange proceeds, even a sense of misplaced priorities in the face of the dazzling foreign reserve are
very genuine. The FMG is advised to take maximum care, plan and
execute projects with minimum delay. With oil and Nigeria, it is
ever the same story of the old farmer's restocking his barns in

the summer. We, like the old farmer, must make hay while the sun shines." (*Nigerian Herald*, July 31, 1974, p. 3.)

21. "Selling [as opposed to the marked] prices of the whole range of goods listed in the P.C.B.'s communique are higher when these items were put under control. With regards to motor vehicles, Mr. Adeyeye ought to know that rises in the cost of accessories (which are not controlled) more than wipe out the forced reductions in the prices of vehicles.

"If, therefore, price control has had only limited impact on controllable commodities, we shudder to think what would happen in the next few months to the more important cost-of-living items such as foodstuffs, rent and transport. It is therefore much more important for government to pay greater attention to these than mere wage rises. Rent in the cities and towns is one of the most intractable problems facing the country. Population drift to the towns simply outflanks all government effort to build more low-rent housing units. Such is the shortage of accommodation that rent edicts have become dead letters. In the long run, a shift in technological processes seems about the best way of reducing the very high cost of housing. Meanwhile hoarding of cement and building materials helps to keep decent housing out of the reach of ordinary workers.

"Transport in the major cities makes a major inroad into the purse of workers. But what is so difficult about subsidising heavily city transport? Workers could for a nominal sum of 50k get a season ticket to use public transport for a month. In a place like Lagos, this subsidy would be a great bonus to workers. In addition, the railway shuttle service between Agege through Iddo to Apapa should be streamlined. A better use of the ferry service could also be made between the island and Apapa.

"As for foodstuffs, the main problem is not so much scarcity but hoarding. Food is fairly cheap now up and down the country, but in a few months the prices are bound to rise sharply, because the traders will have bought and hoarded hundreds of thousands of tons. Hoarders are known in all states but there is little will to tackle them.

"All in all we do not contemplate the arrival of Udoji with particular pleasure. A wage rise is necessary to satisfy the psychological expectation of workers, but provision of cheaper food, rent and social service are more important than isolated wage rises." (*New Nigerian*, November 4, 1974, p. 1.)

22. *Daily Times*, October 1, 1973, p. 1.

23. *New Nigerian*, October 4, 1974, p. 1.

24. On priorities: "As to the most important item of all--
agriculture--we are satisfied that officials have their heart in
the right place but spending must be seen in relation to expenditure on useless projects such as 'cultural' shows and sports fes-
tivities. This raises the question of priorities which will be
central to the success of the whole scheme. Take two items: a
secretariat and a refinery. The way government machinery works
it is just a matter of ticking off progress reports, and if the
refinery is 50 percent complete and the secretariat similarly
placed, then officialdom is quite happy. However, it makes next
to no difference to the country whether a secretariat is completed on schedule. It is this kind of businesslike thinking
which the public service requires and it is hoped that the Udoji
Commission's report will have made its point on the need for
reform of the service." And on the performance ratio: "One fundamental reform of a different kind has been achieved. It concerns the revenue allocation formula which de-emphasizes the
derivative factor. It is a great achievement by the military
administration, and we doubt if any civilian regime could have
achieved so much painlessly. The *New Nigerian* believes that this
measure is in the overall interest of the country. It would have
made nonsense of the federal concept for 10 states to suffer
crippling deficits and two to show confortable surpluses. The
country as a whole will appreciate that the so-called oil producing states are making sacrifices, just as all made sacrifices in
blood for the country to remain one. And blood is thicker than
oil." (Ibid.)

25. Ibid.

26. "The kind of peace and stability which the Commander-
in-Chief seemed to want in his speech on Tuesday is impossible in
a huge and diverse country with fairly well developed political
culture and with the political power prize being the privilege
to dispense vast resources. Turbulence and controversy are second nature to this society. The aim is to control and set a
limit to the degree of turbulence, which is the stuff of politics and the stuff of life. It might be argued with reason that
there are those whose inordinate ambition for political office
will drive them to any lengths to achieve it but there are a
great number among the political classes whose pursuit of power
is legitimate and responsible and it would be a mistake to lump
them all together.

"This latter group will appreciate that at this point in
time it is obvious that the military could not have taken the
necessary steps for a return to civilian rule in 1976, even if
they are responsible for the delay. What needs to be done now
is to expand the base and source of the military's power, by

improving the form of its selected civilian membership and augmenting the substance of their contribution. Civilian commissioners must have some sort of popular backing and the consultative bodies must be allowed to present the genuine feelings of the people. In the past, the regime has frequently been impervious to advice and indifferent to public opinion (e.g. the disposition of governors). This is the right step towards a return to normal democratic government. For the longer the military regime lasts the longer the process of adjustment is put off because by freezing the natural interaction of society's forces you are also freezing the process of political evolution and integration." (Ibid.)

27. *New Nigerian*, January 1, 1975, p. 1.

28. *Daily Times*, October 6, 1973, p. 3.

29. *Daily Times*, December 16, 1974, p. 3.

30. *New Nigerian*, September 19, 1974, p. 1.

31. *Daily Times*, September 20, 1974, p. 1.

32. *Daily Times*, September 16, 1974, p. 3.

33. *Daily Times*, March 17, 1975, p. 3. The editorial added: "We wish to warn that this is a lesson for all of us Nigerians to learn. We should learn not to abuse our official position to amass a fortune. It is a betrayal of confidence. It is illegal. And as and when you are found to have used your official position to amass a fortune, the honourable thing to do is quit such an office. Otherwise the public may be forced to devise means other than the devastating affidavits (now virtually banned) to show their disgust at such an ugly practice. In future, our own public office holders must respect public opinion and be demonstrably governed by public notions of what constitutes departures from accepted norms of morality."

34. Robin Cohen, *Labour and Politics in Nigeria, 1945-1971;* Robert Melson, "Marxism in the Nigerian Labour Movement: A Case Study in the Failure of Ideology" (mimeographed); T. M. Yesufu, *An Introduction to Industrial Relations in Nigeria.*

35. On Decree 21 see Cohen, *Labour and Politics*, chaps. 6, 7.

36. Ibid., chap. 7; Olorunsola, *Societal Reconstruction,* chap. 10. Also see O. Sonubi, "Trade Disputes in Nigeria, 1966-71," *Nigerian Journal of Economic and Social Studies* 15, no. 2 (July 1973): 221-38.

37. *Daily Times*, January 30, 1975.

38. "The Commissioner for Labour engaged in the following activities: He had a chat with labor leaders. 'He did not remind them of the existence of any decree banning strikes and lock outs. He did not threaten them. He appealed for industrial peace. He heard their complaints.' He also met with employers in the private sector. 'He did not order them to implement all the demands of the trade unions. But he told them not to adopt rigid attitudes in their negotiations with the unions. The Commissioner urged those employers who can pay Udoji with arrears to do so in the interest of industrial peace.' On Tuesday, the Commissioner met with leaders of the Central Labor Organization and trade union leaders of the Central Labor Organization and trade union leaders of 28 textile companies in Lagos. On Wednesday, he opened a meeting between these leaders and their employers. According to the labor editor of the *Daily Times*, the labor ministry now acts promptly on matters directed to them.

"The results of these negotiations were as follows: (1) on Thursday 'recalcitrant textile employers who usually rely on police intervention rather than engage in meaningful dialogue gave in. They agreed to pay the new salary scales based on ₦720 per annum minimum. They went further. They conceded arrears effective from October 1, last year.' (2) The union leaders abandoned their rigid position. (3) The 28 textile unions and 28 textile employers of 70,000 workers reached accord. (4) On February 8, 1975 the Federal Government directed that private sector employers should pay three months arrears to workers. The employers agreed." (*Daily Times*, February 10, 1975, pp. 16-17.)

39. *Daily Times*, December 16, 1974, p. 3.

40. *Daily Times*, March 23, 1975.

41. Ibid.

42 "The Nation, The Economy and the Worker: Full Text of Welcome Address Delivered by Mr. G. Kola Balogun on Behalf of the Entire Workers in the Western State to the Wages and Salaries Review Commission," pp. 3-9.

43. *Daily Times*, September 7, 1974, p. 28.

44. *Daily Times*, September 21, 1975, p. 3.

45. Quoted in Cohen, *Labour and Politics*, p. 227.

46. For details of the survey see Cohen, pp. 269-73.

Notes: Chapter Five

1. *Daily Times,* October 2, 1974, p. 1.

2. *Daily Times,* March 20, 1974, p. 3.

3. *Daily Times,* April 4, 1974, p. 7.

4. *Second Progress Report,* p. 103.

5. *Daily Times,* October 2, 1974, pp. 1-3.

6. "Budget Broadcast by His Excellency, General Yakubu Gowon," March 31, 1975.

7. "Leadership and Followship in New Nigeria," *West Africa,* March 25, 1974, p. 354; April 8, 1974, p. 420.

8. *Daily Times,* March 19, 1974, p. 3.

9. Although this is by no means indisputable, the record of past civilian governments would tend to support the military's doubt relative to the civilian's political competence.

10. "Only rich Nigerians who were able to raise bank loans bought most of the enterprises. Mr. G. O. Onosode, Chairman of Nigerian Acceptances, a finance house, spoke of tactics used by some people in privileged positions to acquire shares without revealing the extent of their purchases: 'In the bid to secure maximum allotment, varying tactics were employed, such as changing the profession as well as the order of one's names to produce incredible permutations and combinations and using names of pet animals and procuring domestic servants, 'watch-nights' and secretaries as applicants with a view to consolidating holdings through private transfers, which though strictly legal is contrary to public policy.' The Lagos Stock Exchange did next to nothing to encourage affected firms to sell shares through the exchange. Onosode accused the CIC of 'handing down prices which bore very little relation to either the net asset value of an enterprise or of a business as a going concern.'" (*West Africa,* December 2, 1974, p. 1451.)

11. "Budget Broadcast," p. 6.

12. *Daily Times,* August 28, 1974, p. 3.

13. *Daily Times,* September 8, 1974, p. 3.

14. *Daily Times,* October 2, 1974, p. 1. As a matter of

fact, the life of the military regime is open-ended.

15. "Nigeria is a free country and the citizens should have the right to comment on national issues, including the provisional census figure. . . . We are not yet a police state where freedom of expression would be curbed and I hope we don't become one." (Major General Ekpo, quoted in *Sunday Times*, July 21, 1974, p. 24. "If the generality of opinion is that the military should go in 1976 willy-nilly, programme or no programme, I am sure the military would not overstay its welcome. . . . Those military officers who want to continue at the end of military government should resign their commissions." (Brigadier Esuene, *Daily Times*, July 14, 1974, p. 9.)

16. *Daily Times*, April 29, 1974, p. 29.

17. *Sunday Times*, July 14, 1974, p. 1.

18. *Daily Times*, September 24, 1974.

19. General Gowon, "Budget Broadcast," p. 2.

Notes: Chapter Six

1. This commentary is quite representative: "In spite of its obvious limitations, however, the Second Plan was extended beyond the original plan period of four years to include the 1974-75 financial year. Even then, its objectives were far from totally accomplished. However, as a post-war measure, it did record some notable achievements. For example, it saw the reactivation and construction of a number of infrastructural and other economic development projects like the Nkalagu Cement Factory, the Salt Refinery at Ichoko, the superphosphate plant at Kaduna and the Aba textile mills.

"Others include the extension of domestic air services, the development of existing airports and the promulgation of the Enterprising Promotion Decree which transferred some classified businesses to indigenes of this country.

"Within this period also the framework of the crucial iron and steel industry at Ajaokuta was established, the Marketing Board reformed and Trunk 'B' roads taken over from the states by the Federal Government.

"Thus, the plan could be said to have achieved some measure of success. But it would be wrong to rely on statistics with economic parameters such as the Gross Domestic Product (GDP) and

per capita income to measure the success of a development plan.
At best such data indicate the growth and not the development of
the economy.

"Cardinally, the Second Plan failed to make any significant
impact on the general standard of living of the people. About 75
per cent of the population remain illiterate, unemployment soars
while [the] majority of Nigerians still live at what is inter-
nationally regarded as subsistence level, characterised by poverty, ignorance and disease.

"Our agriculture did not advance beyond the hoe-and-cutlass
technology. Yet the states were unable to exhaust Federal Government facilities for agricultural development simply because
they could not initiate projects that were considered good enough
to attract these facilities.

"The official explanation for these shortcomings is that
the nation lacked the executive capacity to fully prosecute the
projects of the Second Plan. But admission of shortcomings alone
is not enough. Our planners must let the mistakes of the Second
Plan guide them in the execution of the Third." (*Daily Times*,
April 9, 1975, p. 3.)

2. "Budget Broadcast," pp. 2-3.

3. Ibid., p. 7.

4. "Under normal circumstances, prices of perennial crops
like cocoa, palm produce, coffee and copra are announced on the
eve of the harvesting period while those of annual crops like
groundnuts, cotton and soya beans are announced just before
planting actually begins, in order to provide the necessary incentive for the farmers. However, consequent upon recent developments, notably the Udoji awards, and the resultant high increases in general price level, it was decided to fix new producer prices in order to assist farmers.

"The new prices for scheduled commodities will be as follows: beniseed will now fetch ₦264 per metric ton as against the
old price of ₦176; soya beans will be sold at ₦99 as against ₦66;
groundnuts will be sold at ₦250 as against ₦165; cocoa will be
sold for ₦660 as against ₦550; palm kernels will be sold for ₦150
as against ₦132; copra will be sold for ₦200 . . . ; special palm
oil will be sold for ₦280 as against ₦220; technical palm oil
will be sold for ₦265 as against ₦206; arabic coffee will be sold
at ₦700 as against ₦581; robusta coffee will be sold at ₦610 as
against ₦506; while liberica coffee will be sold at ₦565 as
against ₦468.50. The new producer price for seed cotton, Grade I,

has been fixed at 30.8 kobo per metric kilo or ₦308 per ton.

"These new prices represent a mark-up on current prices
ranging from 10% to 50%, and took into account that farmers had
received increased income, since April 1973, with the abolition
of export duty and sales tax on scheduled commodities and the
general upward adjustment of producer prices at the introduction
of the reformed marketing board system. Besides, the prices of
some of the commodities are, for the moment, depressed in the
market. The new producer prices will take effect from the 4th
of April, and will be in operation to the end of 1975/76 season,
in respect of beniseed, soya beans, groundnuts, cotton, coffee,
and up to the end of the calendar year 1975, for copra, palm kernels and palm oil. Buying allowances have also been increased
with effect from the 1st of January, 1975, and licensed buying
agents will be advised of the new rates of allowances." (Ibid.,
pp. 15-16.)

5. Ibid., pp. 4, 6.

6. Ibid., p. 4.

7. Ibid.

8. *The Military Balance, 1974-75* (London: International
Institute for Strategic Studies, 1974).

9. 13.4 percent in the case of the former and 12.8 percent
in the case of the latter (*Sunday Times*, April 6, 1975, pp. 8,
13, 14).

10. Export of traditional commodities amounted to ₦367.8
million in 1970, ₦258 million in 1972, and ₦384.1 million in
1973. But crude oil increased from a 58.1 percent contribution
to total exports in 1970 to 83 percent in 1973.

11. *Daily Times*, December 15, 1974, p. 7.

12. Ibid.

13. A. Sokolski, *The Establishment of Manufacturing in
Nigeria* (New York: Praeger, 1965).

14. Nigeria, Federal Ministry of Economic Development and
Reconstruction, Central Planning Committee, *National Development
Plan, 1962-68*, p. 12.

15. *Daily Times*, April 1, 1975.

16. This was due in part to the euphoric optimism engendered by the sudden "oil boom."

Notes: Postscript

1. *New Nigerian*, August 1, 1975, pp. 8-9; *New York Times*, February 4, 1976, p. 8C.

2. *New Nigerian*, August 1, 1975, p. 9.

BIBLIOGRAPHY

Aboyade, O. *Foundations of an African Economy*. New York: Praeger, 1966.

Adedeji, Adebayo. *Nigerian Federal Finance*. London: Hutchinson, 1969.

Adelman, Irma, and Morris, Cynthia. *Economic Growth and Social Equity in Developing Countries*. Stanford: Stanford University Press, 1973.

--------. *Society, Politics, and Economic Development: A Quantitative Approach*. Baltimore: Johns Hopkins Press, 1967.

Awa, E. O. *Federal Government in Nigeria*. Berkeley and Los Angeles: University of California Press, 1964.

Awolowo, Obafemi. *Anglo-Nigerian Military Pact Agreement*. Ibadan, Nigeria: Action Group Bureau of Information.

Ayida, A. A., and Onitiri, H. M., eds. *Reconstruction and Development in Nigeria: Proceedings of a National Conference*. New York: Oxford University Press, 1971.

Balogun, Kola. "The Nation, the Economy, and the Worker: Full Text of Welcome Address Delivered by Mr. G. Kola Balogun on Behalf of the Entire Workers in the Western State to the Wages and Salaries Review Commission." Mimeographed.

Bienen, Henry. *The Military and Modernization*. Chicago: Aldine-Atherton, 1971.

--------. *The Military Intervenes: A Case Study in Political Development*. New York: Russell Sage Foundation, 1968.

Bell, M. J. V. "The Military in the New States of Africa." In *Armed Forces and Society*, edited by Jacques Van Doorn. The Hague: Mouton, 1966.

Cohen, Robin. *Labour and Politics in Nigeria, 1945-1971*. London: Heinemann, 1974.

Coleman, J. S. *Nigeria: Background to Nationalism*. Berkeley
     and Los Angeles: University of California Press, 1958.

Coser, Lewis. *The Functions of Social Conflict*. Glencoe, Ill.:
     Free Press, 1956.

Decalo, Samuel. "The Colonel in the Command Car." *Cultures et
     Developement* 4 (1973): 765-78.

Dolian, James P. "The Military and the Allocation of National
     Resources: An Examination of Thirty-four Sub-Saharan African
     Nations." Paper delivered at the International Studies
     Association Meeting, March 14-17, 1973. Mimeographed.

Ezera, Kalu. *Constitutional Developments in Nigeria*. London:
     Cambridge University Press, 1964.

Federal Ministry of Economic Development and Reconstruction,
     Central Planning Office. *Second National Development Plan
     1970-74*. Lagos, Nigeria: Federal Government Press, 1970.

--------. *Second National Development Plan 1970-74, Second
     Progress Report*. Lagos, Nigeria: Federal Government Press,
     1974.

--------. *National Development Plan 1962-68*. Lagos, Nigeria:
     Federal Government Press, 1962.

Feit, Edward. "The Rule of the Iron Surgeon: Military Govern-
     ment in Spain and Ghana." *Comparative Politics I*, no. 4
     (1969): 488-97.

Goode, P. J. W. "A Theory of Role Strain." *American Sociologi-
     cal Review* 25 (1961): 483-96.

Gowon, Yakubu. "An Address by the Visitor, His Excellency Major
     General Yakubu Gowon at the 21st Foundation Day Ceremony of
     the University of Ibadan." November 17, 1969. Mimeographed.

--------. "Budget Broadcast by His Excellency General Yakubu
     Gowon, Head of the Federal Military Government, Commander-
     in-Chief of the Armed Forces of the Republic of Nigeria."
     March 31, 1975. Courtesy of the Nigerian Consulate,
     New York.

Helleiner, G. K. "The Fiscal Role of the Marketing Board in
     Nigeria's Economic Development, 1947-61." *Journal of Eco-
     nomic and Social Studies* (September 1964): 606-10.

-------. *Peasant Agriculture: Government and Economic Growth in Nigeria*. Homewood, Ill.: Richard D. Irwin, 1966.

Huntington, Samuel D. *Political Order in Changing Society*. New Haven: Yale University Press, 1969.

Janowitz, Morris. *The Military in the Political Development of New Nations*. Chicago: University of Chicago Press, 1964.

Kilby, Peter. *Industrialization in an Open Economy: Nigeria, 1945-1966*. London: Cambridge University Press, 1969.

Lane, Robert. *Political Life*. New York: Free Press of Glencoe, 1959.

Lewis, Arthur. *Reflections on Nigerian Economic Growth*. Paris: Organization for Economic Cooperation and Development, 1967.

McAlister, Lyle N. *Military and Society in Latin America*. Washington, D. C.: National Technical Information Service, 1970.

Mackintosh, J. P. *Nigerian Government and Politics*. London: George Allen & Unwin, 1968.

Melson, Robert. "Marxism in the Nigerian Labour Movement: A Case Study in the Failure of Ideology." Mimeographed. Cambridge, Mass.: Massachusetts Institute of Technology, 1967.

Olorunsola, Victor A. *Societal Reconstruction in Two African States*. New York: NOK Publishers, forthcoming.

-------, ed. *The Politics of Cultural Sub-Nationalism in Africa*. New York: Doubleday, 1972.

Oluwasanmi, H. *Agriculture and Nigerian Development*. Ibadan, Nigeria: Oxford University Press, 1966.

Onyemelukwe, C. C. *Problems of Industrial Planning and Management in Nigeria*. New York: Columbia University Press, 1966.

Parsons, Talcott. *The Social System*. New York: Free Press of Glencoe, 1951.

Perham, Margery. *Native Administration in Nigeria*. London: Oxford University Press, 1937.

Pinkey, Robert. *Ghana under Military Rule*. London: Methuen, 1972.

Price, Robert. "A Theoretical Approach to Military Rule in New
    States: Reference Group Theory and the Ghanaian Case."
    World Politics 23, no. 3 (1971): 399-430.

Sklar, Richard. *Nigerian Political Parties: Power in an Emergent
    African Nation*. Princeton: Princeton University Press, 1963.

Sonubi, O. "Trade Disputes in Nigeria, 1966-1971." *Nigerian
    Journal of Economic and Social Studies* 15, no. 2 (July 1973):
    221-38.

Welch, Claude E., Jr. *Soldier and State in Africa: A Comparative
    Analysis of Military Intervention and Political Change*.
    Evanston: Northwestern University Press, 1970.

Welch, Claude E., Jr., and Smith, Arthur K. *Military Role and
    Rule*. Belmont, Calif.: Duxbury, 1974.

Yesufu, T. M. *An Introduction to Industrial Relations in
    Nigeria*. London: Oxford University Press, 1962.

Newspapers and Magazines

    Africa Research Bulletin

    Daily Times

    Daily Sketch

    Ghanaian Times

    New Nigerian

    New York Times

    Nigerian Herald

    Sunday Times

    West Africa

ABOUT THE AUTHOR

Victor A. Olorunsola, professor of political science at Iowa State University, received his M.A. and Ph.D. in political science from Indiana University. Born in Nigeria, he has traveled and studied extensively in Africa, conducting research on political recon- struction in Ghana and Sierra Leone as well as in Nigeria. His interest in bureaucracy in developing areas, and in military rule in particular, has led to this book on the development performance of the Nigerian military regime.

In support of his international research, Dr. Olorunsola has been the recipient of numerous grants, including a National Fellowship from the Hoover Institution on War, Revolution and Peace, a Ford Foundation Faculty Research Fellowship, a Social Science Research Council grant, and a grant from the International Development and Research Center of Indiana University.

Dr. Olorunsola has served on the editorial board of the *Journal of African Studies*. His articles have appeared in the *Journal of Developing Areas*, the *Pan African Journal*, *African Forum*, and *African Historical Studies*. He is also the editor of and contributor to the book *The Politics of Cultural Sub-Nationalism in Africa*.

DATE DUE

6-15-77			